RUNNING AWAY TO SEA

By the same author:

Travels by Night: A Memoir of the Sixties
Way Down Deep in the Belly of the Beast: A Memoir of the Seventies
The File on Arthur Moss
Selected Poems
The Dreams of Ancient Peoples
Variorum: New Poems and Old, 1965–1985
Moving towards the Vertical Horizon
Rites of Alienation
Chinese Anthology
The Blue Notebook: Reports on Canadian Culture
Notes from a Journal
The Five Lives of Ben Hecht
The Crowded Darkness
Some Day Soon: Essays on Canadian Songwriters
Year of the Horse: A Journey through Russia and China
Gold Diggers of 1929
The Gold Crusades: A Social History of Gold Rushes, 1849–1929
The Rise of the Canadian Newspaper
A Little Bit of Thunder
The Other China
The Gentle Anarchist: A Life of George Woodcock
Documents in Canadian Art (editor)

RUNNING AWAY TO SEA

Round the World on a
Tramp Freighter

DOUGLAS FETHERLING

M&S

Canadian Cataloguing in Publication Data

Fetherling, Douglas, 1949–
  Running away to sea : round the world on a tramp freighter

ISBN 0–7710–3115–7

1. Fetherling, Douglas, 1949–   – Journeys. 2. Pride of Great Yarmouth (Cargo ship). 3. Voyages around the world. I. Title.

G440.F47A3 1998   910.4'1   C98–931635–1

We acknowledge the financial support of the Government of Canada through the Book Publishing Industry Development Program for our publishing activities. We further acknowledge the support of the Canada Council for the Arts and the Ontario Arts Council for our publishing program.

Text design by Sari Ginsberg
Illustrations by Dallyn Lynde/*Ottawa Citizen*
Typeset in Bembo by IBEX, Toronto

Printed and bound in Canada

McClelland & Stewart Inc.
The Canadian Publishers
481 University Avenue
Toronto, Ontario
M5G 2E9

1 2 3 4 5   02 01 00 99 98

CONTENTS

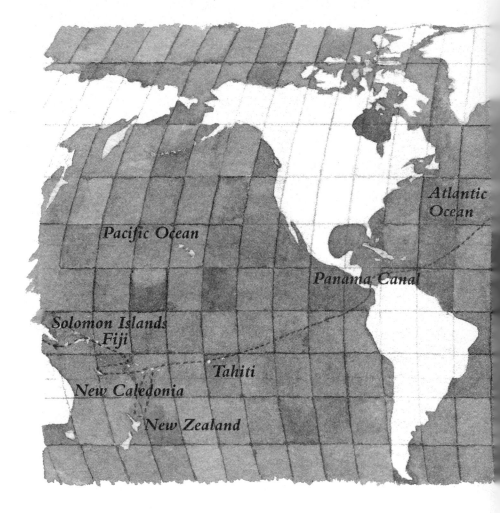

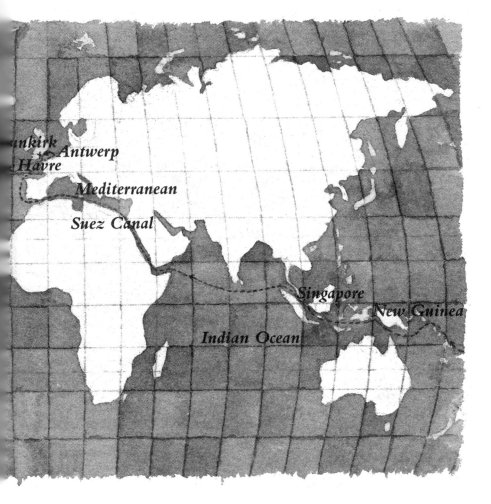

RUNNING
AWAY TO SEA

I

TAKING SHIP

A WEEK OR TWO before I was to leave Canada for England and board a tramp freighter on a voyage round the world, I happened to be down at Toronto Harbour admiring some vessels tied up there. I paid a visit to the harbourmaster, a veteran of the British merchant service with decades of experience at sea. I caught him in a relaxed moment, when there was little traffic in port, and he took a kindly interest in my plans. He asked me the ship's name. When I told him "the *Pride of Great Yarmouth*, out of the port of Douglas, Isle of Man," he tried to look it up in the world shipping directories, which list the 40,000 or so cargo ships in business at any one time. He couldn't find it in the first volume he took down, nor in the second. Finally he located a listing in the third. I could tell that he was trying not to alarm me, but his face took on a worried expression as he ran his finger along the columns of statistical information, which, to a knowledgable user, reveal a ship's entire history and physiognomy. "Oh dear," he kept saying in a soft English voice. "Oh dear, oh dear."

1

Some months before, caught in a quagmire of marital and professional problems, I had decided to run away to sea, after a fashion. I already knew that the three most common fantasies among members of the North American middle class are a) opening a restaurant, b) opening a book shop, and c) going round the world on a tramp freighter. The first of these adventures is almost always doomed to ruin if you're not an experienced restaurateur (or even if you are). A Toronto newspaper tells me of the hundreds of eating-places that start up hopefully in the city each year, only to go quickly bankrupt. Book shops, too, are best left to pro-fessionals. The proprietor of one in my neighbourhood has described people coming into her place of business almost every week, articulating their vision of a dream career. "They think they can sit behind the desk all day and read novels until customers appear with cash to give them," she explained sadly. She added that she dissuades as many of these prospective hobbyist-booksellers as she can, but that some elude her advice and pay dearly for their heed-lessness. That still leaves the tramp freighter trip, an experience that has come down in literature and the popular culture as a passage through time itself, a journey with some (but not all) of the qualities of a religious pilgrimage: a definite belief in the sanctity of process, for instance, but without the devout person's regard for the sacredness of destination. In our imaginations, it has become, in other words, an escape from one place as much as a deliberate attempt to reach another. Was I running away from my difficulties, seeking the time and solitude in which to find solutions? Yes, certainly. I would go alone, as my wife (the bookseller quoted above) declined the offer to accompany me. She couldn't leave her business right then, she said. She also refused to kiss me when I went, saying, "I'm not very good at goodbyes." I said to myself: *Oh dear, oh dear, oh dear.*

When I first laid eyes on the *Pride of Great Yarmouth*, the cargo ship that would be my home for about four months, it looked enormous. The scene of my amazement was a stretch of the docklands at Tilbury in Essex, on the north shore of the Thames about midway between London and the Estuary. This was the place where Elizabeth I reviewed the fleet that set off to fight the Spanish Armada in 1588, but there's nothing historic-looking about Tilbury now. *Decrepit* and *impersonal* would be the words to describe it, even though Tilbury, along with the former seaside resort of Felixstowe, near Ipswich, on the other side of the Thames's mouth, is one of the four busiest ports of the new Europe (the others being Rotterdam in the Netherlands and Antwerp in Belgium). It is easy to believe that Tilbury's inclusion on this list was possible only by virtue of its place on other, older versions of the map. This section of the Thames, lying perhaps 64 to 80 winding kilometres (40 or 50 miles) from the dome of St. Paul's in London, was long the hub of British shipping, the Heathrow of the steam age. A German airborne initiative during the Second World War, however, made it available for redevelopment.

By the 1960s, with the ocean-liner business all but gone and the boom in cruises not yet begun, the place looked a bit sad. I remember disembarking there from one of the last true liners, the Russian ship *Alexandr Pushkin*. In those days one could still feel some sense of London as the commercial capital of the world, but there were also sad old buildings in a state of near collapse. In short, one sensed a dreary contrast between the glory of what used to be and the blandness of what was. By the 1970s and 1980s, however, high-rises had taken up much of the space occupied by the endless piers and warehouses. Then came the container revolution, which reinvented shipping and brought back the bustle to places like Tilbury – once they had retooled to handle the interlocking steel boxes of all different colours that are stacked on a deck like a giant Rubik's Cube. Both Americans and Canadians claim to have invented the now-ubiquitous containers, just as they both claim to have invented the telephone. The *Pushkin*, by the way, ended its transatlantic career two decades later, at the time of the Soviet invasion of Afghanistan, when protesting American dockers in New York refused to touch it. One keeps track of what's become of one's old ships, the way one keeps track of lovers from long ago.

Appropriately enough, it was in this half-light between past and present that I beheld the *Pride of Great Yarmouth*, one of the last of the tramp freighters, though a ship of relatively recent vintage. It was tied up at its berth along a desolate section of industrial wasteland, where weeds grew up between slabs of broken concrete. Hawsers tethered it to bollards on shore. Halfway up these cables were metal disks, like small satellite dishes: rat guards. An ancient jest insists that these prevent land-rats from diluting the gene pool of the ship–rats already aboard.

The *Pride of Great Yarmouth* is of course called that in honour of the seaport in Norfolk, traditional home of the British herring industry. There is, however, no real connection between the vessel and the place. All the ships of the company that owns the *Pride of Great Yarmouth* – for example, the *Pride of Folkestone* and the *Pride of Bournemouth* – are named for cities or towns on the North Sea or the English Channel. Such is the custom of PrideLine plc, one of those slightly mysterious corporations that control much of the world's merchant shipping. The *Pride*s are British-owned, and have British officers, but are registered offshore. This tactic fools no one but the relevant authorities.

Passage on such a ship had been a goal of mine for a long time. In fact, I can date the impulse precisely. Once, years ago, in Vancouver, I experienced a transfixing little jolt of heightened awareness. Out for my daily jog or stumble, I rounded a bend in the Stanley Park Seawall and glanced out at the container ships and tankers riding at anchor in English Bay. There, in the middle of the scrum, was a tiny freighter, ochre in colour and totally obsolete in silhouette. Its superstructure sat amidships, for example, not at the stern, a sure indication that it had been built in the 1950s at the latest. A cat's cradle of booms and cranes was another proof of its seniority, much more telling than the trickles of rust that ran down its side. I stopped in my tracks and stood admiring it for the longest time, thinking of the kind of freighter that Joseph Conrad was forever writing about on terms of such easy familiarity. When I finally decided that the time had come for me to try to put my dream into practice, however, I discovered I was undertaking the project at perhaps the last possible historical moment.

Looking for a ship is less an act than an attitude. It resembles being out of work and looking for a job, or being at loose ends and looking for trouble. The operative word is *looking*, for trying to locate a tramp freighter at this rather late point in our century is like trying to book passage on a camel caravan. Thank God for the Internet. By grappling with its formless masses of undifferentiated facts, I was able to determine that there are four shipping lines still sending tramp freighters more or less around the world: one British, one Belgian, and two German (though operating, in most cases, under flags-of-convenience). I narrowed the focus of my cyber-research and zeroed in on the British company, because it claimed to have a vessel leaving soon for the South Seas via the Panama Canal, returning, eventually, by way of the Indian Ocean, the Suez Canal, and the Mediterranean. That sounded perfect. I was hungry for a ship, and my guardian angel was feeding me one.

This was how I became aware of the *Pride of Great Yarmouth* and its unusual history. As big as it seemed to me when I first saw it tied up, the *Yarmouth* began to shrink alarmingly as soon as I got aboard, as well it should have done. At 160.5 metres (about 530 feet), it was not large even by the standards of ore carriers or grain ships that we in central Canada are used to spotting on the Great Lakes and the St. Lawrence. It was one of two identical icebreakers commissioned in the late 1980s by what was then the U.S.S.R. to equip and supply remote military and scientific stations along its northern coast. Before the last payment was due to the shipyard in Finland, the U.S.S.R. imploded. The new Russian government refused to honour the contract, or couldn't, and the builders arrested – such is the proper legal term – the by-now-completely-fitted-out ships after they had been at sea. The vessels weren't long enough for most purposes and were too narrow to be intermodal container

ships, the kind that now dominates merchant shipping.
A British entrepreneur bought one of the pair (I can't find
out what happened to the other) and had it finished up as
a tramp freighter to carry European goods to Australia,
New Zealand, and the South Pacific and to trade in local
commodities while there. Ergo, the birth of the *Pride of Great
Yarmouth*, strange hybrid. A youngish ship in an ageless, dying
profession. An icebreaker plying tropical waters.

A fact I hadn't quite grasped when I started my research
is that almost everything about the tramp-freighter business
is incredibly frustrating. Because such ships don't have long-
term haulage contracts, they don't operate on what the rest
of the world would consider a precise timetable. They loiter
just outside a port to avoid moorage fees, while hoping that
their agents and sub-agents have found some additional
last-minute consignment. And because they still must
manhandle uncovered cargo on skids for placement
in the holds, they are at the mercy of the weather in a way
that containerized ships are not. If they have, say, sacks of
rice to unload in Singapore and it rains for five days straight,
then they have to sit tight until everything is dry. Accordingly, the departure date I was given turned out to be
maddeningly hypothetical. Some obscure Board of Trade
regulation kept me from occupying my assigned cabin while
the ship was in a British port without a definite time of
departure. As a result, I spent two weeks in a cheap hotel in
London, waiting for the manifest to fill up to the point that
the voyage would go into the black and the owners would
permit us to proceed.

Each morning I telephoned the secretary at PrideLine to
see if there was any news. There never was. I got into the

habit of travelling all the way out to Tilbury every few days
to gaze at the Plimsoll numbers. These are the large markings on both sides of the ship that indicate, along with the
draught marks at the bow, how low the ship is riding
in the water. The name derives from Samuel Plimsoll
(1824–98), "the Sailor's Friend," who campaigned in
Parliament for passage of the Merchant Shipping Act of
1876, which supposedly outlawed the dangerous overload-
ing that had been common practice until that time. Yes, the
signs seemed to show that the holds were indeed starting to
fill, but with agonizing slowness.

I had been getting more than a little impatient at the long
delays when finally, one afternoon, a call to Gillian (the
secretary and I were long since on a first-name basis)
brought the unexpected announcement that the *Pride of
Great Yarmouth* was making ready to get under way. What
had been a tiresome wait suddenly became a mad rush to
get to the dock before the ship left without me.

Given how long we would be at sea, my gear made quite
a load, even though I congratulate myself on travelling
light. There is the matter of clothing, for example. As we
were crossing the Atlantic in September, then getting down
into the tropics, and then perhaps penetrating as far south
as the North Island of New Zealand, I was confronted with
the question of how to dress for both the northern and
southern hemispheres. The solution was a layered look. In
addition to the usual hot-climate garb, I carried a big old
Irish sweater and a roomy Australian oilskin duster with
detachable lining: the kind of stuff that adds a lot of dead
weight. Also, I had made the decision (a tough one) to
severely restrict the amount of reading material I would take

with me. Normally in ten weeks of relative leisure I would probably consume half a hundred novels and other books. But that would have been absurd in this situation. Could I really justify taking even that many smallish paperbacks when I was carrying only a week's worth of socks and underwear? No, I decided; if I had the sudden urge to read something popular, I would have to write it myself. My army-surplus duffle contained only a handful of books, most of them works of Taoist philosophy, the sort of thing that requires concentration and can be read slowly and repeatedly. As I was attempting, with virtually no success, to teach myself Archaic Chinese in order to read the *Tao* in the original one day, I also took my calligrapher's brushes, ink-stone, and hundreds of homemade six-by-nine flash-cards with the characters on one side and their meaning and pronunciation on the other. This way I had more room for such pragmatic items as a mosquito net for my bunk and an extensive but well-thought-out first-aid kit. Under international regulations, freighters must carry a physician if they have twelve passengers. That's why ships like the *Pride of Great Yarmouth* always carry only eleven: in this case, four Britons, a New Zealander, and five Americans, with me, the only person with a Canadian passport, to act as translator (the story of my life). I had no idea how well prepared the others were, but I fancied that I was up to most medical emergencies short of an actual operation, what with ointments and potions, tape and bandages, a range of antibiotics for all occasions, even disposable syringes.

∾

It took forever for the pilot to escort us out of the depressing Thames Estuary and set us free in the English Channel. The Channel smelled overwhelmingly of dead fish and bunker oil, and the clouds in the sky looked like surgical gauze that had started to turn yellow with infection. Yet whatever its deficiencies at that moment, the environment still gave one a robust feeling that the megalopolis never could. I felt like repeating one of my favourite movie lines, when Robert Morley, aboard a pathetic old freighter in *Beat the Devil*, fills his lungs and says with absolute insincerity, "Every breath of fresh air is a guinea in the Bank of Health!" During the long wait in London, I had passed the time going to movies and also thinking about the voyage in terms of its correlatives in fiction and popular culture. That is, I brushed up on my freighter lit, not in an organized way, or even deliberately, but rather as the result of some secret personal imperative.

Robert Louis Stevenson spent his last six years (1888–94) in the South Pacific islands, including Tahiti, where he witnessed three great empires, the French, the German, and the upstart American, jockeying for power in the region. He did not find the spectacle attractive or reassuring. What he liked about that part of the world was that "the nineteenth century exists there only in spots." He meant that the modern age had not totally ruined what he saw, that older local cultures could still be found there. In the same way, I was excited by the possibility of someplace, however tiny and remote, where the *twentieth* century has not quite eradicated all living traces of the nineteenth. Germany lost its Pacific colonies after the First World War (and its African ones after the Second), but the French persist in keeping up the remnants of their Polynesian paradise, though French power ebbed long ago (as the American variety is doing only now). These are some of the facts I hoped to observe firsthand.

Looking at the subject in these terms, I felt that there are distinct French, British, and American traditions in the literature of freighter travel. French writers – the poet Blaise Cendrars, for example – write about freighters with exaggerated romantic relish, using them as retreats from civilization, opportunities to eat bad food, consort with comparative savages, and go for days, even weeks, without shaving: in short, to take a breather from being so obsessively French all the time. By contrast, British authors, it seems to me, especially the great British travel writers such as H. M. Tomlinson (1873–1958), see the freighter as an experience to be endured without complaint, like cold showers at public school, for the sheer moral joy of showing one's superiority over suffering.

Which is not to say that the British are without a kind of black romanticism all their own. I found the following description in *Golden Earth: Travels in Burma* (1952) by Norman Lewis, who to my mind is the most lyrically gifted of travel writers (and who's still at it, by the way). Contemplating a freighter trip, he writes, fills him with

> memories of such rovings, vagrant and obscure of purpose, along the Arabian and Red Sea coasts. The ships had been wonderful, battered old relics, full of nautical mannerisms and impregnated with the musk of exotic cargoes. They had been laid down in ports like Gdynia, with cabins built round the boiler-room in sensible preparation for arctic voyages; and at the end of their lives, when long overdue for the scrap-heap, they had been picked up for a song by

Arabs with sharp trading practices, renamed after one of the attributes of the Almighty, *The Righteous* or *The Upright*, and relaunched upon Arabian seas. Such ships were usually skippered by empirical navigators, captains who lost themselves when out of sight of familiar coastal landmarks. They were nearly as useless as the vessels they sailed in; drank like fishes; went in for religious mania, or for spells of mild insanity in which they were liable to stalk the bridge in the nude. The passengers, too, fitted into the general picture: sword-bearing rulers of a corner of a desert, half-crazed lighthouse keepers, broken-down adventurers scraping a living in any dubious enterprise they could smell out....

With his imagination so equipped, Lewis set off in anticipation of "days of enforced meditation, punctuated by meals taken with some garrulous old salt, delighted to have found so appreciative an audience for his fables." He continued: "It was taken for granted that with the possible exception of a missionary, I should be the only European aboard, but I expected that at the Captain's table I should meet a Chinese merchant on his way to the Mergui archipelago to negotiate for a cargo of edible birds' nests."

Americans approach the subject quite differently. In their tradition, freighters are floating dens of low-life, ignorance, and violence, in which writers (and, vicariously, their audience) can roll about and get dirty – and thus, somehow, with mirror-image logic – cleanse themselves. This viewpoint is expressed with surprising consistency. One example is *Notes from a Sea Diary*, a 1965 work by Nelson Algren, who tramped through South and Southeast Asia on a ship he called the *Malay Mail*. It first seems surprising that this storyteller of the Chicago slums should have been interested in the sea at all (though less surprising, I guess, than the fact that he had a long affair with Simone de Beauvoir – there were obviously sides to Algren that he kept hidden from view). Then one realizes that it's not the sea that appeals to him but its human flotsam. The same holds true in *Steaming to Bamboola: The World of a Tramp Freighter*, the much-admired 1982 narrative by Christopher Buckley, a one-time speechwriter for George Bush. In contemplating the American strain, I make an exception, as always, for A. J. Liebling. His "Westbound Tanker," in the 1944 book *The Road Back to Paris*, is obviously about a tanker, not a freighter, but it captures the down-to-earth romance of the subject. As I recall, so do a few early poems by Gary Snyder, who is only one of many Beat writers of the 1950s to have worked on freighters.

As for Hollywood movies, they add a touch of cinematic evil to the mix. There must be hundreds of instances. I'm thinking, dismally, of Gary Cooper and Charlton Heston in *The Wreck of the Mary Deare* (1959), based on a dreary Hammond Innes thriller. I'm also thinking, more whimsically, of Humphrey Bogart in *Across the Pacific* (1942), in which Bogart's character makes the crossing on a Japanese freighter called the *Geneva Maru*. The character *maru* is still used as a suffix designating Japanese merchant ships, as other cultures use the initials *USS* or *HMS* as prefixes in slightly different circumstances; it means something like "ring" or "sword ring" or "circle crest" – some concept not easily translated into English. In any case, *Across the Pacific* is a little treasure trove of freighter imagery. It is also, by the way, the film in which Bogart (speaking to Mary Astor, who plays a character from Medicine Hat, Alberta) utters the imperishable line of dialogue, "There's a Canadian for you. You

let them take their clothes off and they're happy." (Once
again, context is everything.) Which raised for me the
personal question of how *Canadians* have written about
freighters. It's a point I was a little chary of discussing with
myself, since the example that popped up most readily, the
first piece in Ronald Wright's book *Home and Away* (1993),
was so much more controlled and evocative than anything
I could ever write on the subject that I was almost frightened into staying put and keeping silent. In the end, the fear
of failure wasn't quite equal to the presumption of my
curiosity. But then the whole idea of a round-the-globe
freighter trip is an obvious triumph of immaturity over
common sense. Maybe *this* realization is the Canadian
approach to such things.

In recent years, there has been a boom in so-called
freighter cruises, in which scheduled cargo ships make available well-appointed space for a few pampered passengers
who want to pretend that the old days are still with us and
that they are travellers, not vacationers. This is an idea of
which I am oddly contemptuous. I was looking for a voyage,
not a cruise. What I sought was a working ship, specifically
a tramp. That is, one that sets out knowing its general route
but not its actual itinerary, because it hopes to pick up
as-yet-unknown cargo at various ports along the way and
discharge it at others a bit farther along. The *Oxford English
Dictionary* dates this usage of *tramp* to 1880. The year is
significant, for by then sail had just about completed its
slow cross-fade to the golden age of steamers. Originally,
I believe, the term *tramp freighter* had a happy connotation,
suggesting the seaborne equivalent of tramping through the
fens and dales without a worry in the world. These days

the meaning is closer to *hobo* or even *derelict*, for tramping is a fairly marginal business in an era of monolithic container shipping and fierce competition for air freight. It flourishes (no, that's too optimistic a word) only in out-of-the-way places on the ragged edges of international commerce.

Travelling on a freighter, any type of freighter, is not the same as travelling on a liner. The distinction is fundamental. Liners were fast and luxurious, freighters slow and – if you're lucky in your choice – comfortable. Liners *were*. I use the past tense because liners are of course obsolete as a means of regularly scheduled transportation. A few true liners may survive – the QE2, most famously – but they are no longer a competitive method of getting from one continent to another. To keep up with the times, they have had to become cruise ships: floating resorts. As such, they fight for survival in an economy where shipping is in decline but cruising is very much on the ascent. These days there is even, God help us, a Disney Cruise Line (its motto is "Discover the Magic").

❧

Despite all the delays and bureaucracy involved in our departure, we soon saw the horizon that is France, a dark little squiggle in the distance. In fact, actually getting to France took only a fraction as long as getting out of England, and all eleven of us, the entire inmate population, were gathered at the rail to squint at the spectacle. That done, I returned to my cabin and continued with my unpacking. I paused to read some of the paperwork that the shipping company had been giving me during the weeks before our departure. Just as members of the crew have to sign ship's articles, a contract spelling out their duties and responsibilities, so we passengers had to show acceptance of the "booking conditions." This document takes up four foolscap pages of tiny type. I noted that, in the event of death, loss of limb, loss of eyesight, or permanent total disability while on board, I or my estate would receive £50,000 and that, in the event of hijack or attempted kidnapping, the line would pay to repatriate me back to Canada. I also discovered, in clause 14, subparagraph IV, that the captain enjoys the right to confine a troublesome or dangerous passenger to his or her cabin, or some other room, for the duration of the voyage. This gave me pause.

Gathering at the rail to see France wavering in the distance like a heat mirage on a desert highway provided our first real occasion to get together as a group, for until that point everybody had been busy in the cabins below, settling in. Brief as the Channel crossing was, though, the time had finally come for us to share our first meal on board, before we actually reached Dunkirk. There were no assigned seats in the dining room, so I got to wander in and out of various people's lives and conversations. Doing so confirmed my hasty first impression that the group was more diverse than I had expected: adventuresome business people, holiday-makers, retirees. I appeared to be the only wastrel, though perhaps not the only pilgrim. I was drawn to an American couple in their sixties, Andrew and Judith Murphy of Arizona. Mrs. Murphy, who sported a great deal of make-up, was not, I gathered, a sailor by nature, for I overheard her referring to starboard as "the passenger side." But her husband, a bulky, well-tanned figure, obviously powerful in

his prime, turned out to be a former mariner (many merchant sailors eschew *seaman* and other terms). I had heard
of this phenomenon, of people making good and then
returning to the sea as passengers on cargo ships. They
must be motivated by the same combination of nostalgia
and triumph that provokes former Alcatraz residents to
take the National Park Service tour of their old home.

"I'm here," Murphy said, "because, in all the time I was
at sea, I never transitted the Panama Canal, which had
always been a dream of mine."

He explained that he was once bound for the canal all
right, on a tanker full of naphtha out of Hoboken by way
of Charleston and other southern ports, but he left the ship
before it reached the Zone. Mariners, no matter what their
nationality or the ship's registry, are, by stubborn tradition,
always paid in cash and in American dollars. (One reason, a
minor one, for the resurgence of piracy in the South China
Sea is that freighters' safes are known to contain entire pay-
rolls.) Ship's articles state that a member of the crew may ask
to be paid off at any port along the way and leave the voyage.

"When I was a young fellow, a wise man once told me,
'Always pick a fight with 'em and cash out at New Orleans.
No one's ever had bad sex or a bad meal in New Orleans.' "

Mrs. Murphy frowned, but maybe just because she'd
heard the story many times before.

"Anyway, that's what I did. So this trip here is what you
could call unfinished business."

Murphy, who later went into construction and then
small-scale residential development and then electronic
security systems for the home, had finished his maritime
career as a radio officer. He was therefore known by the

nickname Sparks. On American and British ships, radio officers are always called Sparks (whereas on Greek vessels they are called Marconi). He had accumulated many adventures. Two he told me about.

"I get a call that they need a radio officer in Seattle," he said. "You can't leave until you have one on board. In this situation, the shipping company flies you to the port first-class and sends a limo to take you to the ship. When I get there it's this old – I mean old – hulk. It looks like the last of the Liberty ships. Greeks had bought it and were going to sell it for scrap in Taiwan. But first they would take a cargo of fertilizer pellets to the Philippines."

Individual mariners may sometimes become sentimentally attached to certain ships, but not so shipowners. Vessels frequently change hands – and names and nationalities – because many shipping lines are really in the ship-trading business as much as in the cargo-hauling business, in somewhat the same way that land assembly sometimes seems the main enterprise of the big hotel chains, with hospitality a sideline.

"Well, the barometer drops right off the paper, and the worst storm I've ever seen comes up. And after tossing us around for two days, it leaves us dead in the water. We just sat there drifting. By this time, the boilers are cold. We had a hell of a time getting the engines up." A ship's engines run on bunker oil, while diesel generators run the lights, refrigeration, and so on.

"There was wooden planking laid down on the steel deck," Murphy continued. "As God is my witness, we actually had to start tearing up the planks with crowbars and using them as fuel to prime the engines. We threw in some of the furniture, too. Whatever wasn't screwed down.

But most of this modern stuff" – he pounded his fist lightly on the particleboard table at which we were sitting – "isn't real wood and it goes up in a second, *whoosh*."

Mrs. Murphy was giving her husband a meanly incredulous look that wrinkled her forehead. He saw her reaction out of the corner of his eye.

"Anyway, to make a long story short, we kept breaking down and finally had to be towed into port in the Philippines. The vessel was in dry dock for a month, and we all got a free holiday in Manila on the company. The owners sure didn't make any money on that one."

"Was that your worst experience at sea?" I asked.

He shook his head no.

"The worst was on a big, big ship – thirty-three thousand tonnes or so. We had a cargo of phosphorus and a fire broke out in Number Three hold. Now, you can't put water on a phosphorus fire. It explodes." He raised two fingers of his right hand. "We were just this far away from blowing the bottom right out of the ship, like you'd break the bottom on a beer bottle."

His spouse wanted his attention, so he promised to tell me the rest of the story another time.

We sat in silence for a few moments.

"When you live in Scottsdale," Mrs. Murphy finally said, surveying the view, "you never think there *is* this much water." She added, "Where're *you* from?"

"Toronto," I said.

She looked blankly for a second, as if to say, "Where's that?"

"In Ontario," I added helpfully. But no, I could tell she needed more context.

"Ontario is a province of Canada," I finally said.

She took this in. "Uh-hun."

There was another awkward pause, broken by food and drink, then further conversation. Later, as France got closer, I unsnapped a tiny pair of 8X binoculars from my belt and took a look through one of the waterproof windows. The glasses were of a type, much favoured by birders and whale-watchers, that fold up like opera glasses.

"Those are nice," Mrs. Murphy said, trying to make up for any past suggestion of unfriendliness. "Where'd you get 'em?"

I told her that most outfitters sell them, but that I got this particular pair when I was in Oregon.

"Oh," she said, "is that a Providence too?"

I determined that I would be acting selfishly if I continued to monopolize her charm.

∾

I lost track of time until whistles hooted in deafening triumph or derision as Dunkirk came into sharp focus. A perfectly expressionless *douanière* wearing a crisp uniform waited at the customs shed to examine our passports with a suspicion that nonetheless did not seem to disturb her wonderful listlessness. At this, our first port of call, I expected that most passengers would scurry about buying all the items they meant to pack but forgot or once thought better of. I'm convinced Dunkirk does a roaring trade in such goods. Even at first glance the place looks prosperous, much more so than its opposite numbers on the English coast. This is doubtless owing to its location at the end of the

Channel Tunnel and the general hum of money that seems to pervade the mainland of the European Union.

As we supernumeraries waited our turn to get off the ship and through the gates, a small number of men milled about the dock, hoping to get permission to see the captain. Some were chandlers with order-books in their pockets, should the captain himself need to make last-minute purchases of rope, chain, and other traditional nautical supplies. Farther down the scale were people with duty-free goods to sell at bargain prices, for resale in the ship's slop chest. The slop chest is not as bad as it sounds. It's the little store or kiosk aboard a ship, where officers, crew, and passengers may purchase toiletries, laundry detergent, cigarettes, and liquor. Especially liquor, which drops hundreds of per cent in price as soon as a ship enters international waters, beyond the reach of taxes. *Slop* in this case derives from *sloppes*, those wide pantaloons worn by pirates in old Douglas Fairbanks movies. In earlier centuries, it seems, the master of a vessel kept a chest of clothing from which he would supply his men, at a personal profit to himself, of course. This monopoly has grown into the present system, in which the captain and perhaps other senior officers jealously guard their privilege, even though they no longer profit from the sales as individuals. The slop chest is opened or closed at the discretion of the master, who on some ships keeps the only key on his person at all times. This is because, in extreme cases, captains have been known to use the slop chest as an innovative management tool. The sea tends to attract hearty, self-educated individualists. When such crew members grow especially cranky, or when their thoughts turn to voting, a wise captain will sometimes take out the key to the slop chest and let vodka douse the flames of dissent. This calls for fine executive judgement, of course.

Also spotted on the dock was the shipping agent, who was welcomed aboard almost at once. The holder of this wonderfully Conradian job title is central to the smooth operation of any merchant-shipping enterprise. Just as in Daniel Defoe's time, there are special agents, who represent only one line, and the more common general agents, who handle business for a variety of owners. The man hurrying up the gangway was a general agent. He came to deliver and receive messages, arrange for new crewmen whenever someone decides to cash out, and to keep the vessel supplied with victuals and all other staples. More important, he helps to find the clients who wish to consign cargo to some port or other. Here in Western Europe this usually means loading up with manufactured goods for various buyers in the Western Pacific. Once we reached the islands, I was told to expect that the agents generally would be harried-looking East Indians with cellphones and pagers, operating out of third-floor rear offices in stuccoed side streets close to the harbour. In such places they are approached by planters with crops going to market. A prosperous general agent will always have a ship arriving soon from somewhere en route to wherever it is coconuts are to be auctioned. He is a matchmaker, for cargoes instead of couples.

We lay overnight at Dunkirk and then, the next morning, with the air clear and our senses adjusted, we began to chug down the coast to Le Havre, where the Seine enters the ocean. A couple of days later, we would be heading across the Atlantic. I would not set foot on land again until we reached Papeete, the capital of Tahiti, which I calculated to be at least 14,400 kilometres away (about 9,000 miles).

2

PANAMA

$\mathcal{T}$HE *Pride of Great Yarmouth* is not the fastest ship afloat. Many of the specialized container ships and tankers built in recent years are capable of about 33 knots, which is to say 33 nautical miles an hour. (A nautical mile equals 1.852 km or 1.15 land miles.) The next generation of Japanese ships poised to come into service can do 50 knots, meaning that under ideal conditions they could cross the Atlantic from New York to London in about 62 hours. Cargo ships, built for heavy loads but not necessarily urgent ones, are much slower. Their typical speed is probably 15 knots, meaning (again, in perfect circumstances) that it would require 33 hours for one of them to travel only 500 nautical miles. The *Pride of Great Yarmouth* supposedly boasted a top speed of little more than 17 knots. Hidden in its contracts with the people consigning cargo to it is a magic number, privileged information unknown to me, below which its cruising speed must not fall. The penalty is to be declared "off hire," like a taxi returning to the garage. To continue with the taxi metaphor, if this occurs, the meter is turned off and the customer doesn't have to pay until it comes on again. So, even on a tramp freighter like this, whose very being suggests a less-harried attitude towards commerce, there is always pressure on officers and crew to keep up a good steady pace and avoid costly mechanical delays. Everybody is kept hopping.

There are no cabin boys any more. The lowliest member of a ship's company is the wiper, who works in the engine room with oily rags, cleaning up after the oiler, who is hired to keep the engines lubricated; both are filthy jobs. Just as in earlier days, however, the backbone of the crew are the able-bodied seamen and the ordinary seamen, called ABs and ordinaries. An AB is supposed to have studied engineering and be capable of taking the helm if need be (though he is not schooled in navigation, which is the preserve of officers). An ordinary, for his part, is a crew-man who has not yet written his AB examination. Both categories work on deck under a bosun, who is not merely a foreman but also a kind of shop steward, representing the crew's interests to the officers. The crew of the *Pride of Great Yarmouth* numbered twenty-eight, far fewer than would have been required even a few years ago. Such is the effect of advancing technology.

For reasons I couldn't at first explain, all the *Pride of Great Yarmouth*'s crew on this voyage were Russian, or at least Russian-speaking, for some had Ukrainian-sounding names and I had reason to suspect another of being a Pole. The composition of the crew had a great deal to do with world politics. A decade ago, such a group would have been more polyglot. Undoubtedly it would have included some Bengalis, some Pakistanis, maybe some Somalis representing Africa.

Often there was a lonely Burmese, afraid to return to his ever-more-repressive homeland. Now events in the former Soviet Union – the necessity of either joining the new spirit of capitalism or getting trampled and left to starve – have filled the world's sea lanes with Russians slaving for the coveted U.S. dollars with which they may one day return and open a small business. Just as the Revolution of 1917 left Paris, London, Shanghai, Rio, and other major metropolises with blocs of White Russians, driven into exile by communism, so now the counter-revolution has created communities of exiled former Red Russians, condemned to nomadic behaviour by the urgency of change.

Some will never make it back home. In today's maritime environment there are said to be Russians who rarely stay on land very long but travel the world in engine rooms, listening to their savings accumulate in the ship's safe and dreaming their melancholy and sometimes melodramatic Russian dreams. In Patagonia, I'm told, there is a sort of colony of Russian mariners whose exact population is constantly turning over. Manning agents who are seeking crews all know it well. It is the sort of place where there is always some engine utilityman, sobering up and with his toolbox out of hock, willing to take on the worst possible job on the least desirable ship. Some of the Russians aboard the *Pride of Great Yarmouth* seemed quite infatuated with the West, others not. The most westernized one, curiously, was one of the few who spoke no English whatsoever. She was Marina, one of the "stewardesses," who patterned herself on Marilyn Monroe. She made herself up to look like Marilyn Monroe – same hairstyle, same peroxide, same makeup – and she had the body language and the breathless voice down perfectly, too. "Is it my imagination," Sparks would ask one day after we had been at sea a couple of months, "or are her heels getting higher and her skirts shorter?" I told him I wasn't sure about the shoes. Whenever I saw Marina, I kept expecting her to sing "Happy Birthday, Mister President!" But she never did. She just giggled in Russian.

If my calculations were correct (arithmetic is not my forte), we would reach Panama in about twelve days. In that time, the passengers would come to know and then probably dislike one another, and all of us would have built some sort of social relationship with at least a few of the officers, as the passengers and the officers took their meals together. But the crew saw little of us, or we of them. A few of them barely saw daylight. The class divisions on a working ship are absolute and inflexible. The chasm would be observable through binoculars from a great distance, the officers in their crisp white uniforms with brass buttons, the crew in greasy coveralls or track suits and running shoes. Many crew members wear hooded sweatshirts with the Batman logo or other pop-culture symbols. They sleep four to a cabin in what is still called the fo'c's'le, where they spend most of their limited free time gambling, fighting, and swapping untruths. Every now and then some bit of improper behaviour has to be noted in the captain's "wet log" – "wet" in this case meaning official. Sometimes a member of the crew is mentioned with the polite notation *NFFD* – "not fit for duty." On rare occasions, when the offence is serious and has come to the attention of the authorities in one port or another, the log will indicate *FWE*. This means "finished with engines," denoting that a ship has completed its voyage. When applied to individuals, however, it means that they have been dropped from the crew because, for example, they've been jailed on a drug charge and won't be returning from shore. Authorities in American ports, I am told, believe that Russian mariners show a special propensity for attempting to smuggle hand-guns into the United States, weapons that end up on the New York black market. The pistols are called "dogs" (or rather, DOGS – a Russian acronym I don't understand). In effect, they are single-shot 12-gauge shotguns in hand-gun form. They look like homemade flare guns, but are stronger and carry enough kick to knock down the shooter as well as the target. These weapons are made in cellars in Moscow and St. Petersburg, with profits returning to the Russian mafia. Mind you, I'm not suggesting that such activity has ever taken place on the *Pride of Great Yarmouth*. For one thing, none of the ports it touches is exactly a smugglers' paradise, not unless someone has figured out a way of dealing in illicit peppercorns at Vanuatu. I mean only that life below decks has its own code and its own secrets. At least that's the impression we were given.

I was misinformed in first thinking that there was no physician aboard. One of the passengers turned out to be a retired surgeon from London, a small wizened man, precise and even fussy, but funny as well. He was travelling with his far-better-preserved wife, a severely upright woman with neatly trimmed vowels. They seemed an odd pair, he a *Guardian* reader, I am certain, or so he would have others believe, for he was of the right age to have been a very young socialist at the tail end of the 1930s. By contrast, she clearly had been a *Daily Telegraph* person since birth.

At breakfast, they told us about life during the Second
World War.

"I was a medical student," said the doctor. "I can remember dissecting a cadaver at St. Mary's, Paddington. The operating theatre was illuminated partly by large dormer windows. We could look up and actually see dogfights taking place. Battle of Britain."

He waited for the rest of us to react to this macabre image.

His spouse chipped in: "I was living in Leeds during the war. Even there you weren't always safe. Sometimes the German bombers, if for some reason they couldn't reach their targets, would just dump their bombs anywhere. That way they saved enough fuel to get back, you see."

Such talk seemed fitting. We had just come from Dunkirk, where we saw the beach where the British army had been trapped and had to be rescued by the legendary ad hoc fleet of fishing boats and other small craft. And we were only a day out of Le Havre, whose architecture is chillingly postwar for the most part, because the city was so heavily damaged in the Allied rebound later on. Yet this couple were the oldest passengers on the ship, and their tales proved amazing to the New Zealander in her early twenties, who was returning home after several years' work and schooling in Belfast. To the horror of the English couple – you could read the reaction on their faces – the young Kiwi really didn't know anything about the Second World War, except that it came after the First, at some point in history, long ago in geological time. She had an untroubled expression and a cheerful manner and was wearing a sweatshirt advertising Otage Ale, although with her

Pre-Raphaelite features she would have looked perfectly in place in Victorian attire. In fact, she appeared at times like a minor character in a Merchant Ivory film.

Among the others at the long table, with its extra-heavy chairs designed especially for rough weather, were a woman from Denver, who read Stephen King novels and listened to New Age music; a fitness-crazed former career officer in the U.S. Navy; and two middle-aged women travelling together, the one English and the other a Scot, both enthusiastic knitters and cribbage players. In terms of the passengers' ages, I fell somewhere in the middle, but I was far older than any of the crew, or even the officers. We had acquired a new master at Le Havre. He was forty-two. At that same port we had also taken on a new officer cadet, an Irishwoman of only twenty, who was determined to work her way up the system and make a life at sea. Her presence was a refreshing sign, as the world of merchant shipping is as exclusively male as it is heavily weighted down with questions of rank and class. "I'm glad they've done away with that old business of a captain having to go down with her ship," she said with a mischievous wink.

The ship makes two complete circumnavigations a year. On the previous voyage, I am told, the cargo that was picked up at Dunkirk included two racehorses bound for Le Havre. They were hoisted aboard in nets, heavily sedated, each accompanied throughout the eighteen-hour run by its own veterinarian (meaning that there were then two doctors on call). This time out we had left Dunkirk and Le Havre with steel beams, frozen chickens, chocolate, rebar (tons and tons of rebar), and a few French automobiles. At Le Havre the dockers had spent an entire day and much of an evening off-loading a 52.5-metre (175-foot) barge to us. It was stacked with 40-kilo (88-pound) sacks of flour, on open pallets, bound for Tahiti.

❧

Once out to sea, we started to feel like passengers on a tiny iron wafer being tossed about by the elements; the westerlies across the top of the Bay of Biscay made for choppy water, to say the least. From the stern I could make out a Norwegian tanker that had been following us at a prudent distance since our last port of call (as though it hoped we knew the way). A walk up to the bow proved difficult. A large-diameter pipe, used to heat fuel slightly to make it flow more easily, ran along the port side of the ship. This system wasn't working as it should have been when we tanked up, and an air bubble formed in the hose. As a result, three and a half tonnes of oil had spilled onto the deck. The crew went to work with high-pressure hoses, scrapers, brooms, mops, and pails, but the decking was still slippery and gooey. In addition to such permanent obstacles as the type of black bollards known as elephants' feet, the deck was littered with scrap lumber, bits of tarpaulin torn away in the wind, lengths of chain, coils of rope, piles of rags, and a mysterious pine box that looked, alarmingly, like a coffin (but couldn't have been – could it?). I climbed over all this, working my way towards the bow, as the ship bucked like a wild animal trying to bound its way through a deep snow-drift. When I arrived, I hung on for dear life as the sea crashed over the gunwales, putting in my mouth a salty taste, which I discovered was somewhat addictive. The wind was a deafening whistle that changed pitch as it blew round the cranes and through the small stacks of containers on deck. In fact, I quickly learned the reason that portholes are made as they are, with double-thick safety glazing and big rubber gaskets: not only to keep out moisture, but, just as important, to shut out the constant racket that accompanies every involuntary movement of the ship, day and night, hour after hour.

One morning I was awakened by all the doors and drawers in my cabin opening with a creak and then slamming shut again as the sea played with us. First the drawers in the dresser came out, one by one, top to bottom. A few seconds later they slid back into place in reverse order. This was followed by the drawers in the desk. I lay awake in my bunk for an hour, determined to ignore the ruckus. Finally I got up and sealed everything in place with duct tape. (Travel tip: Always carry a roll of duct tape. A thousand-and-one uses.) So when the fire alarm went off at 0500, I slept right through it. Most of the other passengers seemed to be stirred to action, however, and so they were more cross than confused when a second bell started ringing two hours later.

This one I heard. After a poor showing at a lifeboat drill our second day out in the open Atlantic, I wanted to perform well, so I was dressed and ready, with my filthy life-jacket securely tied and its little light and whistle in the proper places in the webbing. I was about to ascend to the prearranged muster point when a Russian sailor, unshaven, sleepy-looking, and in greasy white overalls, said to me, "Not real. Return to sleep, please."

The *real* drill, a memo later informed us, would be at 1030 hours, after everyone had had breakfast and coffee.

By this time, I had begun to regret my harsh judgement of Mrs. Murphy. I originally thought she was rude or stupid. In fact, what distinguished her, rather, was her absolute mastery of malapropism. Her casual way of mangling the language and garbling clichés would challenge even the great Samuel Goldwyn of Hollywood legend. With the ship still pitching and yawing at breakfast, and bits of scrambled egg falling off people's forks, she opined that we were probably in for much worse later on, once we entered the Pacific.

"This is just the tip of the X-ray," she said.

An unfortunate choice of words, we all seemed to be saying to ourselves, as jars of Robertson's marmalade went rolling up and down the table.

❧

The ship's toilets hadn't worked in two days. An engineer called to investigate was baffled. Better the toilets than the engines, he said. One had to agree. Finally, a much-more-lowly member of the ship's company, a Russian electrician with a most unusual nickname, Lucky, was able to solve the problem. He also did good service in fixing the clothes dryer. This machine had gone on the blink moments after I completed my first load of laundry. With everything still dripping wet, and having with me nothing I could use as a clothesline, I took the laces from my shoes, tied one or two items of clothing to each, and hung them out the porthole to dry in the wind. I was in a race against mildew. The method, though somewhat labour-intensive, worked well enough, and my apparel had a fresh, salty smell. I couldn't just spread the stuff out in the sun, because every metal surface of the *Pride of Great Yarmouth* was covered with either oil and rust or soot from the stacks.

We had been at sea for only a short time when certain facts became evident. One was the change in the water itself as we crossed the invisible line beyond which the Atlantic becomes the Caribbean. If you were to try to paint a picture of the Atlantic at that time of year, you would want to begin with Prussian blue, very deep and serious. As it got warmer, the water took on a pigmentation closer to cerulean blue. Tinges of green also started to appear. Another thing I noticed was that the other passengers were already at one another's throats. On the surface, at least, the problems had to do with food. When I first learned that I would be on a vessel with a Russian cook (rather, Ukrainian), I assumed that we were in for four months of borsch, boiled potatoes, and really delicious bread, still warm from the oven. In fact, the menu was devised, and its execution closely supervised, by our long-suffering purser, an Englishman from Luton. What we received was British cuisine as interpreted by a Ukrainian, hardly the best of both worlds. One day we were served some quite peculiar sausages that I identified as bangers and mash *à la russe*. No one smiled at my witticism. At that point, the British passengers and the American ones would have removed to separate tables were the other table not reserved, by custom if not by edict, for the captain and his chief engineer (who was, inevitably, a Scot).

The Americans – Sparks Murphy and his wife the mala-propist, the New Age woman from Denver, a raspy-voiced female freighter junkie from the Midwest, and Tim Beneke, the highly likable former U.S. Navy officer, now in civilian electronics – complained constantly about the Englishness of the cuisine. Or all of them did except Tim, who seemed pretty cosmopolitan and sophisticated. The others prattled on endlessly about how the flavour was cooked right out of all the dishes, which therefore didn't taste American, and about how they kept getting stuff put in front of them that they'd never heard of. What the hell are diced swedes? they growled. And bubble and squeak? Is this what you people mean when you say pudding? One of the "Brits" was always explaining, saying, "Try it, you'll find it quite tasty really." Mrs. Murphy drove some of us batty by always saying "Cornish pastie" instead of "Cornish pasty." One day, when she had forgotten to bring her spectacles, I read the menu aloud for her, and inserted something about "Cornish pastie with G-string potatoes," but she didn't catch on.

The Russian servers possessed limited English. The British passengers – the retired surgeon and his wife and the two retired ladies having the holiday of their dreams – ordered by pointing politely to the name of each item on the photocopied menus and saying, "Savoury chicken with processed peas, please," or whatever. The Americans pointed but also spoke very slowly and VERY, VERY, LOUDLY, so as to penetrate the language barrier. The Russians rolled their eyes as they took the orders; they also looked sad, with the great sadness of the ages.

The dilemma, and it had become quite severe, was that the Americans by and large found the British stuck-up, effete, pretentious, inefficient, old-fashioned, and over-civilized. For their part, the British believed the Americans – though they were too polite to say so to their faces – were a wild and noisy and unpredictable people, given to vulgarity and unusual Christian names such as Joleene and Xrystal-Lynette. The way each group used a knife and fork made the other cringe and affect the look of someone suffering the side-effects of dental surgery. This left only me and Molly, the New Zealander (whose paternal grandfather immigrated there from Ireland in 1914 aboard one of the first ships to transit the Panama Canal).

There was a time when I simply would have sat with the English and the Scots and thought no more about it, as I was something of a lime-juicer in my younger days. Now, in my middle years, I'm far more tolerant. Even of the New Age priestess, who said "Tootles" instead of "Goodbye" and insisted on volunteering information about her finances (such as the fact that, while she was away, she put all her business affairs into the hands of her massage therapist, the only creature she trusted, other than her cats, Agent Scully and Agent Mulder). I believed it was imperative that I remain as neutral as possible, because first I found that I had to look out for Molly, whose vocabulary needed translation of some kind, and second I really enjoyed the company of Tim.

Tim got out of the forces in the late 1980s after putting in his twenty years. Many career military people come away from the experience more rigid and narrower in outlook than they were when they went in. But some, like Tim, seem to emerge with their horizons broadened, their curiosity permanently aroused, and their patience rendered inexhaustible. Tim came up through the ranks, being commissioned from chief petty officer, the hard way. As though to clear the air about a question hanging unasked above us, he volunteered the information that he had done two tours of duty during the Vietnam War. The second one was uneventful, he said, but the first was cut short by a tragic accident. In 1967, he was serving on the aircraft carrier USS *Forrestal*, which had five thousand officers and men.

"We were making an alpha strike," he reminisced darkly. "That's when you put into the air everything that can fly. The second aircraft to take off had a malfunction. It just blew up. This sent a bomb down through the flight deck, where it detonated. Then there was a real domino effect: explosions and fires went round the deck, with one aircraft setting off the next, and so on. We limped back to Subic in the Philippines, fighting fires all the way." About 140 people were killed. "Our efforts to contain the fire were filmed. The footage is still part of the standard Navy training film on firefighting, even today. As recently as a few years ago, I saw it in some documentary on the Discovery Channel."

Everyone at the table fell silent. Tim cleared his throat. Believing that he now had to say something to justify his participation in the war, he told us, "The average age was just nineteen, but I was an old man, getting on toward thirty. I thought then and I think now that it was a useless and senseless effort."

I for one was embarrassed that he apparently believed he had to announce this in front of strangers at this late date, but I didn't know how to express my feelings. In the end I just found myself quoting General Charles de Gaulle's remark about the French phase of the war: "It is a dirty business on both sides." Everyone seemed to sigh in relief, and the group moved on to other topics.

Although this was hurricane season, we managed the Atlantic crossing without encountering dangerous weather (or, rather, by assiduously stepping out of its path). One morning, however, we did experience unusual turbulence. Aboard ship, as in a prison, feeding time presents the greatest danger to order, because it is the only point at which all the inmates are gathered together in one place. Visibility outside had dwindled from only ten nautical miles to barely three; inside, dispositions were correspondingly cloudy. The passengers almost came to blows in a heated discussion about, of all things, ice cream. The Americans ground their teeth when the British spoke of "lollies," a word not included on the official vocabulary list with which all Americans come equipped at birth. The Americans then boasted of their own national achievements in ice-cream technology, which, to judge by the tenacity with which they adhered to their convictions, seemed inextricably bound up with the blessings of democracy itself. I said that in my experience the Russians make the best-tasting ice cream, but that its extra-high butterfat content means that it's also the worst, medically speaking. This innocent observation caused sparks to fly all around, and I privately resolved to shut up before being asked to. Molly unwittingly resolved the tension by claiming that the world's best ice cream, as everybody knows, was hokey-pokey-flavoured, and found only in New Zealand.

"What the hell's hokey-pokey?" an American demanded.

"A dance craze of the forties, as I recall," said the woman from Scotland.

"Naw," said Molly. "You know, it's the hokey-pokey. The stuff that they put in vaniller ice cream."

"But what is it exactly?" asked Tim, very scientific in his method of enquiry. "I mean, is it candy of some sort? Dried fruit?"

"Naw, it's just the hokey-pokey. If you haven't had it, then nawone can explain it to ya."

We debated this from several points of view, including the existential and the quietist, and people left in a better mood than they had come in. Noting what had taken place, however, the captain, who was not a social man by nature, decided that he should throw the passengers a cocktail party in the lounge, followed by a cold buffet. This proved a pretty dismal affair, organized by the already overwhelmed purser. The officers were dressed in their whites, the captain in trousers, but the first officer, who had the key to the fridge, in Bermuda shorts. People introduced themselves to the captain, who seemed disappointed with the low turnout among the ship's officers, and asked each guest what he or she would have to drink. If one answered that a beer would be fine, the captain said "Beer!" and the first officer turned the key and extracted a can from the fridge – then locked the door again. An officer cadet circulated with a silver tray of barbecue-flavoured crisps, which were stale.

As I slipped out of the room and returned to my books, I passed a pocket of the party where the subject under discussion was global warming. As I went out into the companionway, I overheard Mrs. Murphy expressing her personal anxiety about how aerosol cans were eating a hole in the Stradivarius.

And so to bed.

∾

Every day at precisely noon, two officers would step out onto the bridge and make separate calculations as to how far the ship had travelled in the past twenty-four hours. This procedure was already a tradition centuries ago when the simplest sextants were used. The difference today is that, in order to arrive at "observed distance," the two navigators factor in the number of revolutions the propeller has made and the amount of fuel consumed, so as to know, at any given time, the projected profit or loss on the voyage thus far. Their figures, along with notations about the wind, sea, and visibility, are entered in the captain's log and then into the daily log abstract that is left for the chief engineer outside the door to his cabin.

At noon on the first day that I witnessed the ceremony (we were by now approaching Panama) the observed distance was 412 nautical miles. By normal standards, this would not necessarily be a poor showing. But we had been retarding the clocks by one hour each night for several evenings, as we'd passed through different time zones. We had therefore been operating on twenty-five-hour days, so that the log was weighted slightly in our favour. Even making allowance for the 4-per-cent distortion, we still needed to make up for lost time. The scuttlebutt told to me by the twenty-five-year-old second mate from the Midlands was that, if we didn't hurry, we could possibly lose our place in a convoy going through the Panama Canal and be forced to ride at anchor for several days in Panamanian waters until we earned another spot in the queue. In practical terms, this would mean that we passengers would probably get some time ashore in Panama, which is a remarkable zoo of human behaviour, or at least was when I visited in the 1980s; signs at the casinos requested that gamblers check their handguns on entering. In any case,

Panama would certainly be no less symbolically interesting, even if we didn't get ashore – even if, as seemed likely, we were to pass through the canal at night. The policy at the time of which I speak was to give the daylight hours to vessels carrying hazardous or potentially hazardous cargo, ships such as LNGs, liquid natural-gas carriers. As we didn't yet fully understand what we were carrying, this news was pretty hard on Sparks Murphy, whose presence on the *Pride of Great Yarmouth* was expressly for the purpose of going through the canal. I suggested that maybe he could resort to one of the increasingly popular three- to eight-day cruise packages that cater to tourists. "One of them promises 'Christmas on the Isthmus,'" I said hopefully. Sparks growled at me.

As it happened, we got to the canal on schedule, 484 years to the day after Vasco Núñez de Balboa (c.1475–1517), a thirty-eight-year-old adventurer, completed his trek through the jungle from the Spanish colony of Darien, on the Atlantic coast, and laid eyes on the Pacific Ocean – the first European ever to do so. Balboa's "discovery" of what he called the Mar del Sur set in motion five centuries of jockeying, warfare, confrontation, and exploration by assorted Europeans and later Americans, an epoch that is only just now experiencing its final death twitches.

From the Caribbean to the Pacific, the Panama Canal, one of the world's great engineering megaprojects, runs about 80 kilometres (52 miles), takes in swamps, three sets of twin locks, one of the world's largest artificial lakes (Lake Gatun, formed by a dam across the River Chagres) and, most remarkable of all, the big ditch called the Gaillard Cut, a path through the Continental Divide hewn out of solid rock, 13 kilometres (8.1 miles) long and 150 metres (165 yards) wide.

The idea of cutting through the narrow strip of land separating North and South America was first articulated at the Spanish court only ten years after Balboa, when the long and dangerous alternative route, through the Strait of Magellan at the tip of South America, was itself still a new discovery. The canal proposal was turned down, however, at the urging of the king's theologians. More than three hundred years later, such dreams were revived, once gold had been found in California, and argonauts, as they called themselves, hurried to the Pacific Coast from New York or Boston via steamers to Panama, and then alternately hacking and paddling their way across it. In the Pacific, just as in the Atlantic, gold has often been the motivation for European policies and migration, for it was the French, successors to the Spanish in much of the world, who talked most actively of building a canal through Panama. They made some progress under dreadful conditions after first opening a transcontinental railway there when the California gold rush was coming to its greedy conclusion.

The French plan came from Ferdinand-Marie de Lesseps (1805–94), the diplomat, engineer, and promoter, who, starting in 1859, had built the Suez Canal. He gained fame and riches in the Near East, though he found himself bogged down in litigation and a growing list of restraints, some having to do with his use of *corvée*. Politics aside, though, the Suez Canal, massive as it was, presented nothing like the challenge of a cut through Panama. The Suez was and is a sea-level canal, in effect a simple ditch linking the Red Sea and the Mediterranean. Now Lesseps

proposed the same type of canal between Colón on the
Caribbean and Panama City on the Pacific, a path that
included all topographic extremes, from marshes to mountains, was covered in dense rain forest and criss-crossed
with unpredictable streams and rivers. Huge mud slides
were another problem. By announcing that he would build
such a canal and offer shares to investors, Lesseps stole a
march on other dreamers with different designs and other
proposed routes. He promised completion in twelve years,
but was soon a full year behind schedule; he was also well
into his seventies. He began speaking of fundamental
changes, making the canal a series of lift-locks. Too little,
too late. The company went into bankruptcy, and a French
court later convicted Lesseps of stock fraud. When the
United States declared war on Spain in 1898, the assistant
secretary of the navy, Theodore Roosevelt, wrung his
hands as one of his warships took two months to travel
around South America to Cuba from California. In 1901,
when he became president, Roosevelt pushed for an all-
American canal. Again, various routes were discussed, but
the chance to buy Lesseps's partial canal for only US$40
million forced a decision.

Creation of the Panama Canal, indeed of Panama itself,
was to some extent an American covert operation, as we've
learned to say today. Panama was only a province of Colom-
bia until 1903. Then Washington bankrolled the Panamanian nationalists, who succeeded in setting up their own
breakaway republic, and then, the following year, signed an
extraordinary treaty with the United States. The agreement
established the U.S. Panama Canal Zone, a right-of-way
extending eight kilometres (five miles) either side of the

canal; the Zone would be U.S. territory, under American law. Not since the creation of the treaty ports in China had a guest country actually declared a part of a host country an extension of itself, in perpetuity, no less.

The canal-building took ten years and cost the lives of twenty thousand workers, mostly Caribbean and Asian labourers who died of yellow fever and malaria. Construction was completed in August 1914, the month the world went to war. More than a thousand ships used the canal in its first year of operation; now about fourteen thousand move through it annually, forty a day. The commonest cargoes are grain from Europe and North America headed for Asia, and automobiles bound from Japan to North America. Containers and petroleum products come next. A single one-way transit of the canal itself usually takes at least nine hours, not counting the wait at the entry point. Vessels too big to use the canal are said to be "overpanamax." The *Pride of Great Yarmouth* had plenty of room to spare, being almost 120 metres (400 feet) under the length limit; and with our beam of 24 metres (80 feet), we would have nearly 4.5 metres (15 feet) of clearance on each side going through the locks. Ships that fit in length and breadth but draw too much water when full sometimes off-load part of their cargo so they will temporarily fall within the draught limit of 12 metres (39.5 feet).

The canal has undergone numerous improvements through the decades, just as the original 1903 pact has been tinkered with almost from the start. But the Americans would never allow the main point, absolute American suzerainty, to be readdressed. This rankled with generations of Panamanians, and pressure built. In 1965, Panama City, the only metropolis, was almost torn apart by anti-American riots, and Panama cut diplomatic relations with the United States, in effect blackmailing that country into agreeing to some major treaty modifications. From that point on, the politics grew even sleazier – on both sides.

In the late 1970s, General Omar Torrijos Herrera of Panama's National Guard seized power in a coup d'état, setting the country on a leftward course that found little sympathy in Washington. This is the General Torrijos whom Graham Greene tried to present, in his book *Getting to Know the General*, as a charismatic figure. Finding a Democratic Party interregnum to the north, in the United States, however, the Torrijos government concluded a treaty with the Jimmy Carter administration in 1977 that committed the United States to turn over the canal and the Canal Zone by noon on December 31, 1999. This agreement was arguably the second most important factor in Carter's defeat in 1980, after his failure to free the American hostages in Iran (whose Shah, by the way, found sanctuary in Panama). Subsequently, Torrijos died in a mysterious plane crash (which Greene and others believed was the handiwork of the CIA). He was succeeded by General Manuel Noriega, whom we now know to have been in the CIA's pay when that organization was under the direction of George Bush. Noriega abolished the National Guard and created what he called Dignity Battalions in its place.

With Torrijos dead and Carter turned out of office, Noriega became the inevitable focus of American dislike of the new treaty (which was ratified by a referendum in Panama and of course only by Congress in the United

States). This was the situation in March 1989 when the Panamanians caught an American spy, one Kurt Muse, in the act of setting up a network of clandestine radio and TV transmitters, installations that were but one part of Washington's plan to rig the outcome of the Panamanian elections scheduled for May. Later it was revealed that George Bush, by then president, had personally appealed to the CIA to provide more than US$10 million to help defeat its old contract agent, Noriega – whose name the American press habitually prefixed with the phrase "Panamanian strongman," as though he were an attraction in a carnival sideshow.

As it happened, though, the scheme of George Bush was only a faint shadow of that dreamed of by his predecessor. Ronald Reagan, the American strongman, had sought to topple Noriega through the diplomatic equivalent of sending Panama to Coventry, and then through economic boycott, the bully's favourite toy. Before the process was quite complete, however, the United States indicted Noriega on drug charges, in absentia, of course. When Noriega refused to co-operate in his own incarceration, the White House proposed getting rid of him. Not necessarily in terminal fashion, but rid of him in any case. The customary army of exiles, trained and funded by the CIA, was poised in Miami, ready to strike. The plot faltered, not because the government was overcome by an unexpected wave of morality but rather because it feared getting caught again. Bush's plan, at the time of the 1989 election, was more benign.

Noriega was no better and no worse than the standard Central American military type, attempting to keep his country together in the face of enormous American pressure (such as was even more obvious in Nicaragua at the time) and, in the process, to keep himself lucratively positioned in the seat of power. Harmony would have been better served if Washington had simply let the rascal be. Instead, the Americans sent an invasion force to Panama (Operation Just Cause), kidnapping Noriega and bringing him to the United States – not for ransom, but rather to serve time as, in his own words, a political prisoner. His term is forty years. Another part of the invasion plan called for Delta Force, the combined special-forces unit, to rescue Kurt Muse, the CIA spy, from the notorious Modelo Prison (which the current president of Panama, Ernesto Perez Balladares, known as El Toro, ordered to be ritually dynamited in December 1996 – a gesture as symbolically rich to Panamanians as the storming of the Bastille was to Parisians in 1789).

At post-invasion staffing levels, 10,000 or 11,000 U.S. military personnel were stationed in Panama. Slowly, the troops have been withdrawn. The figure is now fewer than 6,000 and falling. The assorted forts and air bases, indeed the entire Canal Zone, are being handed over to the Panamanian government, which is frantically trying to convert the real estate into enterprise zones and recreational facilities. USSOUTHCOM, the headquarters for all American military operations south of Mexico, has left Panama for Miami. The military especially mourn the loss of Fort Sherman, their school for jungle warfare.

The shipping community grows increasingly sceptical of Panama's intentions with regard to the canal itself. Will the facility continue to be maintained with American-style efficiency? Will tariffs continue to rise as service declines? Meanwhile, inside Panama, others ask what the effects of all the sudden redevelopment will be on the environment and on the native peoples. There were sixty tribes in Balboa's day. Now there are six, the largest of which is deadlocked in a land dispute with the government. Indigenous people have tended to support President Perez Balladares's market-oriented wing of the Revolutionary Democratic Party over the anti-American wing led by Geraldo González (whose son was charged in the killing of an American soldier in 1992, on the eve of a visit by President George Bush). But such support seems to be waning. Indeed, González may be the new president very soon, if he is not already in power by the time you read this. You see, the people of Panama love the Americans, who once employed as many as 7,500 people on the canal and whose local military expenditures once amounted to 5 per cent of Panama's gross domestic product. Still, they hate them too.

Some insist that the Panama Canal has had its day and should be abandoned. Others believe it can still compete, even in the face of possible rivals. Japan and Taiwan, the two richest nations in East Asia, both major players in all facets of the shipping industry, have talked of financing a new and bigger canal to the south. Brazil, Bolivia, Argentina, Paraguay, and Uruguay are putting forward a plan to blast a channel from the Atlantic to the South American interior by changing the course of the Paraguay and Panama rivers. The waterway, 3,500 kilometres (2,175 miles) long, would cost at least US$1 billion. It would also probably destroy the Pantanal, the largest wetland in the world.

In an ironic twist to this entire situation, the United States has made a new deal with Panama, promising to come to its defence if necessary. For the Panamanians now have the problem of protecting their windfall – presumably from their traditional enemies, the Colombians. The danger comes not only from Bogotá's government troops but also from Colombian insurgents who raid across the border into Darien, which contains some of the planet's most inhospitable jungle. Significantly, the Pan-American Highway, which otherwise runs from Alaska all the way down to Tierra del Fuego at the bottom of South America, has never been pushed through Darien, the place from which Balboa struck out overland across the isthmus.

"All I know," said the second officer of the *Pride of Great Yarmouth*, "is that the past couple of years when we've got the pilots, who are always American, to take us through the canal, they've had Panamanian trainees with them, learning the ropes, you might say."

I asked, "How do these new people impress you, professionally speaking?"

"Unfavourably," he answered. "Very unfavourably indeed."

❧

After thirteen days at sea, including six days without seeing another ship, our first glimpse of land came at 1730 hours. The mossy green Panamanian headlands appeared some distance off the port side, just as the sun began to set, rather spectacularly, off starboard. One of the strange facts about an Atlantic-to-Pacific transit of the Panama Canal, which is by far the more common direction to travel, is that one enters from the northwest and exits at the southeast. This is hard to imagine without referring to a map, yet absolutely true. With darkness descending quickly, we anchored outside the Cristóbal seawall to await developments in the morning.

We had a reservation to do the deed twenty-three hours later. Such reservations are optional. They are also, we were told, often meaningless, especially at such a time as this, when one side of the double locks is closed for maintenance, so that the other side must be used, on an alternating basis, by ships heading in both directions. Sparks was optimistic that we might begin earlier than expected and so do most of the trip in daylight. In the evening we saw numerous other vessels all around, some done up with so many lights that they looked like offshore casinos. In the morning, however, with the sun up and the lamps off, they were revealed as just so many merchant ships like ourselves – freighters, container vessels, tankers, of all sizes, nationalities, and creeds, from 125 to 1,000 feet (approximately 38 to 300 metres), Chinese, Mexican, American, Norwegian. One could go on. We eleven passengers were fully awake at first light, but the *Pride of Great Yarmouth* was not. It seemed to be sleeping in. Then, slowly, and with much starting and stopping, it entered the gap in the seawall and took its place in Límon Bay, the Panama Canal's anteroom. I counted thirty-nine other ships there.

Getting ready to go through the canal is an ordeal for the officers and crew. For two successive nights, our captain ate his dinner on the bridge, standing up. The purser was run ragged, preparing all the paperwork, which covered every horizontal surface in his office on the poop. At one point he came to collect passports and health cards, in order to compile a list for Panamanian immigration officials. Molly revealed that she didn't have a health card, which shows that the bearer has been

inoculated against cholera, typhoid, and assorted fevers. The
news threw the normally unflappable purser into a tizzy.

"How did you get on board without a yellow card?" he
kept asking her. "You can't land without your yellow card."

After a couple of hours, however, the crisis subsided. No
one was talking, but my guess was that the purser had prevailed upon the elderly London physician to produce a
plausible-looking document for his young fellow passenger.

In the early afternoon, two inspectors from the Panama
Canal Commission radioed ahead to ask the *Pride of Great
Yarmouth* to lower its aluminum ladder on the port side and
prepare for their arrival. While the captain, first officer, chief
engineer, and others waited with anticipation to receive
them there formally, the PCC tug pulled up at starboard,
coming from aft where no one could see it. The invisible
inspectors kept shouting for admittance. Finally their presence was discovered, a Jacob's ladder was rolled down the
side like a carpet, and the inspectors came aboard, all pocket-
protectors and clipboards, wearing mismatched pieces of
fancy military-style uniforms. A few more hours passed, and
then came the Panamanian pilot, who would stay on board
until we reached the Pacific. The purser had been preparing for the pilot's arrival, making sure the spare cabin was
ready. The pilot's prestige is such that, like a rock star's, his
agreement specifies that he shall be provided with a dress-
ing room stocked with certain delicacies. The pilot also
resembles a rock star in that he arrives with an entourage.

In all, fifteen Panamanians were in the party. "Like
pirates," Sparks said derisively. "For a minute there, I thought
we were going to have to repel boarders." By now, he was
in a foul mood. It was already 1700 hours and he knew that

the daylight wouldn't last much longer. Crew members, too, were openly contemptuous of the locals, having painted white footprints on the deck plates, quite unnecessarily, I am sure, to show them which way to go. But the purser told me that, for all the obvious overmanning ("Socialism, that's what it is"), the Panama Canal is not burdened by the kind of graft that is part of the system in the Suez Canal; there is no complicated tribute in cigarettes and booze every time a task needs doing or a form needs to be signed off. One of the Panamanians who was supposed to be learning the piloting business, however, did go about the ship trying to sell plastic hammocks. He had few, if any, takers.

After what seemed interminable delays, the engines started again with teeth-rattling assertiveness and we were slowly under way, a tugboat at our side like a border collie, nuzzling us this way and that. In the distance loomed the free port of Colón, a long line of low buff-coloured build-ings with red tile roofs, a silhouette broken by a few high-rises and one twin-spired Spanish church. Behind the town spread ranks of darkly verdant mountains. Between city and mountains, in the middle distance, emissions from some industrial plant made hash marks on the sky. The shoreline was surprisingly empty and impenetrable-looking; sailboats and catamarans curtsied against a backdrop of palms. Our crewmen were hopping now, sliding down stairway-ladders using only the handrails, with no time to put their feet on the steps. We passed them on our way to the monkey island, or flying bridge, where we could enjoy the best view.

The first thing we noticed up there was that the engines weren't performing perfectly. Huge, awful plumes of thick oily smoke, the kind that would choke an ox to death, were coming out of the stacks and polluting a large patch of sky everywhere we went. None of the other ships we had seen was having this problem. Downwind of the funnels it was actually difficult to speak, so foul and sooty was the air. We all moved as far forward as possible.

One of the engineers was there, surveying the jungle scenery, and I asked him what the trouble was. "Obviously we're not getting a clean burn," he said. Even I could have figured that out, given my expert knowledge of what I am sure Mrs. Murphy would call the internal commotion engine. "Too much air in the mix, I would guess. It's been getting steadily worse since we left Dunkirk." Then, as though to put our minds at ease, "I know that up here it must look like the pair of 'em, but I assure you it's only the starboard engine that's wonky."

A second discovery took our breath away in a more fig-urative fashion. One of the two masts on the monkey deck was flying the flag of Panama as a courtesy; below it were two coloured pennants indicating the two-digit number we had been assigned while awaiting our turn (pick a number – like a bakery or a deli). The other mast flew a company flag, and then the red Bravo signal flag. Flying Bravo is the international symbol that means dangerous cargo onboard. We were shocked. I went off to find some officers and ask what exactly warranted such a signal, but they refused to say. They would concede, under my grilling, only that it was neither radioactive nor biochemical in nature. "Oh no, nothing like that, or you would have been told," they assured me. Talking among ourselves, we passengers finally con-cluded that it was probably explosives for use by one of the extraction industries – the gold mines in Papua New Guinea or, more probably, the nickel mines in New Caledonia, the world's third-largest producer of nickel (after Canada and Russia). Off to starboard, storm clouds were building like a bad mood.

Approaching the first set of lift-locks we passed almost within lip-reading distance of other ships heading in the opposite direction. Along with its suddenness, such proximity is also the most intriguing aspect of using the canal. Without warning, the immense prow of some vessel will appear silently from a bend in the channel and slide past you like an enormous steel dinosaur. We arrived at the Gatun Locks at 1830. Night had fallen, but the three steps of the locks were brightly lit by powerful lamps on high standards. By their glow, we got a detailed look at the strong, squat locomotives that, by means of lines thrown around the elephant's feet on our cargo deck, pulled the ship along. The locomotives, three on each side, ran on a single track up a series of steep inclines. Mrs. Murphy said it looked like "a Ferris-go-round." She meant a roller-coaster. And she was right. It also reminded me of a funicular railway, such as those in Quebec City or Pittsburgh. Under the light globes we could also see patches of the lock where the concrete had crumbled away, exposing the reinforcing rods. Nothing that looked too serious, yet hardly confidence-building.

With a tug nosing us into the narrow entrance, we were following one lock behind a much larger ship named the *Tigris*. We entered and water was pumped in until we had risen 25.5 metres (85 feet) over the course of the three stages. This sounds simple, and looks simple on paper, but much of the night was gone before we were into Lake

Gatun. Here all was darkness except for channel markers and other navigational aids. The lake was large enough that we could traverse it at up to eight knots all the way to the Gaillard Cut, which ends in the other two sets of locks, the Pedro Miguel and the Miraflores.

As we had become accustomed to rising at five in the morning on this voyage, we tended to disappear from the monkey island one by one, giving in to the magnetic pull of our bunks. Finally only Sparks Murphy was left. He told me at breakfast that he had stuck at his self-assigned post until the ship passed under the Bridge of the Americas and entered the Pacific at about two-thirty in the morning. When he said this, he was still in a state of repressed euphoria. The rest of us were groggy. We were riding at anchor, within sight of the bridge and the skyline of Panama City, waiting for the bunker to pull alongside and top up our fuel supply with about a thousand tonnes of Texaco. I had heard that the company liked to avoid buying oil or services in Panama if possible, because prices are inflated. But this voyage, I was learning, was not necessarily routine. The storm clouds we had seen forming the previous night had arrived. The bosun and his crew pulled on rain slickers over their greasy white boiler-suits as they began to pump the fuel aboard.

3

SOMEWHERE IN

THE PACIFIC

*W*E HAD PUT Central America behind us and were making, with all possible haste, for Papeete, the capital of Tahiti, in French Polynesia, 4,491 nautical miles from Panama (itself 4,772 nautical miles from France). Barring the unforeseen, we would arrive in about thirteen days. The effects of the warmer water were immediate and salubrious. During the Atlantic crossing, for example, the arthritis in my right knee had given me a bit of trouble, a fact that did nothing to make me more nimble as I navigated about the rolling ship; I had more bruises than a barrel of apples. (Memo: When I get home, I must see my palaeontologist for a check-up.) A day earlier, the New Age guru from Denver had cut open a piece of fruit and discovered an insect inside. It scurried away before she could stop it. She told us ominously that it was an omen. Yes, I said, a portent of imminent infestation. So it proved to be. Suddenly the ship was full of roaches and strange little beetles, glossy black and perfectly round, each the size of a shirt stud. At about this same time, the Russians played a prank on

Molly, the naïve young New Zealander, giving her big tumblers of vodka instead of water. She'd never tasted vodka before, and swore she didn't have a hangover on this occasion, though her eyes were red and her skin ashen. "I've never had a hangover in me whole life," she said. "Mind, I am feeling a bit *fazed*." Meanwhile, Mrs. Murphy returned from a hard afternoon's sunbathing to announce that she was "overcome with heat prostitution." Indeed, the weather was hot and lovely during the day, and interesting at other times.

Two nights running we saw beautiful flashes of T-shaped lightning, accompanied by thunder and squally rain. The first such storm caused enough roughness for small light objects that were not weighted down to go flying about the cabin. At one point, the atmosphere recalled *The Amityville Horror*. The second storm was conducted in stillness. At one point the diesel generator shut down; for a few moments, the strobes of lightning were the only illumination in the cabin. When dawn came, at five-thirty or so, it seemed nothing more dramatic than the night unravelling.

Deep-water ships take a terrible beating from salt and rain and just plain hard use. The *Pride of Great Yarmouth* had rust streaks running down from giant bolts and rivets like stigmata, and there was about it a general air of decrepitude. With the weather improving, the ABs and ordinaries turned their attention to cosmetic and maintenance matters. Bare-chested Russians scraped and painted various surfaces. I saw one fellow perched precariously on the gunwale of the starboard lifeboat, with only the sea beneath him, painting the davits with a long-handled roller, much as one would paint the ceiling of one's apartment. Ship's chores, like housework, are unending, but this was a particularly fine day for such activity. Notwithstanding the occasional rogue wave, the sea was steady, with only spindrift washing the bow and dripping down inside the hawsepipe. Our bow-wave looked perfectly formed, as the prow cut a wide furrow through the water; our wake was long and wide, like a deserted avenue leading backwards in time to the horizon. Yet nothing was quite so idyllic as it seemed. Up on the navigation deck, Hamish, the ship's computer genius, a twenty-eight-year-old Scot with a gold ring through his right nostril, had been having difficulty with the ship's telecommunications. For telex and voice contact with head office in London (a different matter entirely from navigational equipment), the ship was using satellite time from a new supplier, Saturn M. "Named after the Roman god of frustration," Hamish quipped. The connection had not been working at peak efficiency since the voyage began. At best, one could sometimes get an anaemic phone hook-up, but only one party could talk and be understood, and then only for a few seconds at a time. Hamish, incidentally, got his position in part because he could read and speak Russian. All the ship's software manuals were in Russian, and he was slowly translating them. A valuable crew member.

Down in the bowels of the ship, what, in land terms, would be four storeys below, the twenty-five-year-old fourth engineer had been struggling for three days to get one of the purifiers working. The ship had bunkered up on fresh water at Le Havre, for domestic purposes and for use as a coolant in the engines. In the first case, the water passes through a purifier attached to the diesel-electric; in the latter, there are two much larger purifiers connected to the oil-burning engines. The water in Le Havre is quite hard, and even in so short a time as this, enough scaly mineralization had built up inside one of the main purifiers to shut it down. If left unchecked, the situation could have led to one of the engines seizing up, in which case we might have had to limp into a port somewhere, depending on what the bean counters in London decided (assuming that Hamish could reach them). If both engines seized, we would have been shut down at sea for emergency repairs, the voyage most emphatically in the red. Fortunately, there was absolutely no indication that this would be in our future any time soon, if at all – though by this point the fourth engineer had taken apart the equipment, cleaned it, and reassembled it a half dozen times.

On its last voyage but one, the *Pride of Great Yarmouth* went halfway round the world on only one engine, doing twelve to fifteen knots, on a trip that was intended to last 110 days but ultimately took 158 – so long a time that many of the crew demanded to be paid out at Singapore. The company, of course, made no profit on the venture. That was also the passage during which the supply of domestic water closed down and passengers had to raid the drinking-water rations in the lifeboats. The deck crew hauled seawater in buckets in order that the toilets could be flushed. I asked if there was at any time the danger of running out of food. No, I was told. Unfortunately not. (Russian humour.)

Throughout the trip I thought and wrote a great deal about how I might repair the damaged marriage I had left behind me in Toronto. I couldn't send faxes and could receive them only occasionally, when climatic and electronic conditions were right; the ones that got through seemed to me colder and sharper as the voyage proceeded. I could make telephone calls, however, from many of our ports of call, but these didn't always go well, either. One night, as I lay in my bunk, which was about a foot too short for me, I remembered how sometimes back in Toronto on a cold winter's night, our large dog, Dexter, would appear suddenly in the bedroom doorway and ask if he could come up on the bed with my wife and me. When he stretched out between us, careful to make contact with the human on either side, I would lean over and put my ear on his upper body, listening for his heartbeat. This was a little ritual we had. A ship has a heartbeat, too. I would roll over in my kip a few inches and put one ear to the bulkhead and feel the vessel's whole circulatory system pumping away. Sometimes the pulse became irregular, which jarred me back into complete wakefulness. Occasionally a quite different sound was carried up the steel framework. I can't describe it except to say that the ship seemed to be chuckling softly to itself.

As we neared the Equator, we passengers spent many productive hours squabbling over the remains of a newspaper. When the official Panama Canal pilot, his task completed, had disembarked and returned to his office in Colón, he left behind in his cabin a copy of the previous day's *Miami Herald*, "international edition." One of our Russian stewardesses (again, that's what they're called) found it near the bunk, and we passengers passed it among ourselves, one section at a time. Not much of a newspaper, it seemed to me. None of the seven stories on the front page had originated in-house; they were all from wire services. The paper did, however, publish a generous section of shipping news, the sort of stuff to which I recently had become attuned. I gobbled up information about trends in break-bulk cargo-handling or the latest wrinkle in the Jones Act (the law requiring that U.S.-flag ships be used for carrying cargo between consecutive U.S. ports). The ravenousness with which we all devoured this stray newspaper showed the extent of our isolation. Had it been only three weeks since I was in London, watching, as the world watched, the funeral procession of Diana, the Princess of Wales? Half a globe away, I felt as though I hadn't had any fresh world news in absolutely ages and, of course, no Canadian news at all.

All the nine occupied passenger cabins had telephones, but only one of them had a dial tone. This was the one in the cabin of Tim, who discovered that it actually worked, sort of; that is, it worked for intramural calling only. As an experiment, he tried phoning the purser, two decks below, for some tonic and other mixes, but instead got through to the captain on the bridge, who probably jumped a foot, thinking that head office in London had finally reached him via satellite. There were short-wave radio receivers on board as well, but despite some artfully improvised antennae they produced nothing but static for all of us except the doctor. His surgeon's fingers seem to be able to coax a faint signal from the BBC World Service for a few minutes every few days. Whenever he had some information, he saved it for the dinner table, where he suddenly became the star.

One night he told us that the smoke from enormous forest fires in Indonesia had so reduced visibility in the Strait of Molucca, through which we would pass on our way home, that two freighters had collided. One sank in only a minute. Rescuers were still searching for twenty-nine people who were unaccounted for. This provoked a discussion of shipboard safety (and plans for a beefed-up session of the weekly lifeboat drill the next day, when the exercise scheduled was "mock-rescue of fourth officer from fire in confined space"). In turn, this led to talk about the shipping industry as a whole. The captain was nowhere in sight, so some junior officers felt free to speak of such matters.

"Standards are going down all the time, because crews are getting smaller and smaller," one explained. This is caused partly by a corporate desire to save money by abolishing positions and ordering senior officers to perform more of the duties themselves, using new technology. "The Old Man these days has to be a computer wizard and all," said another of my informants. "And let's face it, he's way up in his forties somewhere." Too old a sea dog for such new tricks, it seemed.

"There was a time when you'd stay with one company for years," another piped up. "But now shipping is like other industries. They don't wrap you in cotton wool for your whole career any more, do they?" Officers and crew now are virtually all pick-ups, hired through offshore staffing agencies, which do the recruiting and assembly of person-nel; all the shipowner has to do is submit a list of require-ments. For the *Pride of Great Yarmouth*, the British nationals were engaged through a firm on the Isle of Man, the

Russians through one in St. Petersburg. Everyone, regardless of rank, is on contract for one voyage at a time, and contract employees may be let go at any point, for any reason,
with two months' notice or the equivalent in redundancy
pay. The British officers are members of NUMAST, the U.K.
transport union, while British ABs and ordinaries belong to
NSU, the National Seamen's Union, the British equivalent
of the SIU, the Seafarers' International Union in the United
States. NUMAST does not bargain collectively for the
officers' salaries. What it does do, however, is pay the legal
bills of members who are implicated in accidents and other
mishaps at sea and must defend themselves in admiralty or
civil courts. The NSU is a bit perkier. Indeed, it had a
reputation for mild militancy during the Margaret Thatcher
era, when trade unions felt themselves under constant attack
from the government. By the standards of many other old
industries, however, it is a pretty timid union. Even in the
United States, where the SIU's reputation for toughness
and tenacity made it feared as a kind of seagoing version of
the Teamsters, the mariner has historically been low on the
social and legal scales. Flogging was not prohibited on U.S.
merchant ships until 1850. As late as 1897, the federal
Supreme Court ruled that the Eighteenth Amendment to
the Constitution, the one outlawing slavery and other
involuntary servitude, did not apply to merchant sailors.
The ruling stood until 1915.

And the work is dangerous (even when the ship is not
flying Bravo). Showing off my new-found interest in industry matters, I pointed to a statistic from Lloyd's that effec-
tively stated that five hundred merchant ships a year are sunk,
wrecked, or otherwise lost at sea somewhere in the world.

"That sounds like a lot," one officer said. "Of course, they're probably counting anything of a thousand tonnes, or even less."

"Mind you," another pointed out, "our fleets in Britain and Europe may be downsizing, but look at the Far East, where just the opposite is happening. Tremendous growth. I wager we'll probably *see* five hundred ships in harbour at Singapore."

"And Lloyd's estimates," I continued, "that a hundred of the five hundred losses are scuttled for the hull cover." That is, insurance fraud.

"Now *that* I can believe," replied one of my interlocutors, first looking over his shoulder. The others nodded in agreement. Everyone laughed. Then the tone of seriousness returned. "If I were starting out today," said the original speaker, "I wouldn't go to sea. There's just no future in it." The person saying this was probably not yet thirty.

Everybody on the ship works a seven-day week, except the cadets, who get one day off to study their textbooks in navigation, mechanical engineering, and other technical subjects. The second-hardest-working members of the company are the two cooks, who bring new meaning to the term galley slaves. They prepare all the meals for the dining room and for the two messes – the Mess and the Dirty Mess; the latter is where crew eat who haven't yet changed shifts and cleaned themselves up and are still likely covered in grease and oil. The hardest-working of all are the three Russian stewardesses, who serve all the meals to officers, crew, and passengers and also clean the passenger cabins and common areas every day. When they work the dining salon, they are expected to wear starched white blouses and long black skirts, even at breakfast. They even have to wear heels, no matter how rough the sea. Once they finish serving breakfast at 0830, they are allowed a coffee break, before they change into jeans, sweatshirts, and bandanas (and running shoes) to Hoover the carpets, scrub the lavatories, change the bed linen, and bring everyone fresh supplies of ice and drinking water. This occupies them until lunch is served at noon. What with their own nutritional requirements and the fact that dinner begins at six, they have only two free hours during the day. During this part of the voyage they used the time to get into their swimming suits and sunbathe together up near the bow, hidden behind a privacy screen of deck cargo. They all had rich, deep tans. Their evenings were free to clean their own cabins and do their laundry and ironing.

Each of the stewardesses was assigned a certain number of passengers, whose feeding and looking-after were her responsibility for the balance of the voyage. Mine was named Olga. Olga from the Volga, some of the officers called her, though the Volga is nowhere near her home in Novosibirsk in central Siberia. She had a gold tooth at the front of her mouth and wore a small silver crucifix. She was thirty-one and had a husband and son back home. She was trained as an art teacher, but complained that she couldn't find a position in that field. She might get some better job in trade or tourism if she could master English, she explained. (We conducted our conversation partly with signs, gestures, and pantomime.) She said, "I am sick for home. Is that what you call it? Yes. Ship cannot end for me too soon enough." Sometimes I heard her complaining, in Russian, to the stewardess who looked like Marilyn Monroe. I don't know the language, but I understood the drift. Olga was accusing

Marilyn of flirting with the passengers and officers instead of pulling her weight. But this seemed to me an unfair suggestion, at least as I observed events. No doubt the jobs came with a great deal of stress.

As for the passengers, with one or two exceptions, they really didn't like one another, and such feelings seemed to deepen as time went on and we racked up distance. Despite this, I managed to get us all together for a meeting in the lounge to discuss gratuities for the cooks and stewardesses. For anyone besides an officer, tipping is allowed. Indeed, it is customary, for the pay is miserable. I researched the subject with the purser and the master and was told that the going rate for rewarding the cooks and stewardesses is US$1.50 a day at sea for each passenger, to be split 30 per cent for the cooks and 70 per cent for the stewardesses. I managed to get everyone present to agree to continue the practice. The only modification I suggested was that we pass the hat at the end of each month, instead of only once, at the completion of the voyage. There was consensus.

Our first month was short, as we didn't put out to sea until the eighth. On the thirtieth I did my calculation and figured that we owed them for twenty-two sea-days at US$1.50 times eleven passengers, which equalled US$363. Some people only had sterling or francs, so, as in a Monopoly game, I seemed to end up being the banker. Finally I got all the exchange complete. When I did, 363 American dollars seemed an even more pitiful amount than I had first imagined, but I knew that it was worth much more in Russia than it was out here, or indeed in a great many other parts of the world. The only problem, explained the purser, was that they had no secure means of sending it home. Russian banks and wire-transfers were not to be trusted. And neither was the post. The purser didn't know what the male cooks did, but he said the stewardesses had told him that, when the voyage is finally over, in Europe somewhere, they take their salaries and tips, converted into hundred-dollar notes, and stuff their underclothes with them. "Even then," he said, "they all travel together on the train back through Russia. Sometimes the Russian mafia hold up the train. The poor people can't win."

∾

The rest of us on board continued to be nonplussed by Molly's easy command of New Zealand patois and Mrs. Murphy's gift for malapropism. One evening, the chief engineer, who claimed to have a certificate in cocktail technology, mixed a bloody great vat of the vodka punch for which he said he was famous in some jurisdictions, notorious in others. The impromptu party, which followed a poker game, went on into the warp of the evening, when the sea got too rough for the revellers to continue. Molly had last been seen on the bridge, draping herself in the New Zealand ensign, after someone had broken into the flag locker. Even after the event she claimed that her nationality or genes, or both, gave her unlimited immunity from hangovers. The next morning, however, she did have to excuse herself from callisthenics on the monkey deck, saying she had "a touch of the dry horrors."

"I had those once in the Dry Tortugas," I said. But no one was in the mood for repartee of this calibre.

At 0830 hours most of us were only half awake, if not because of the party, then because it had been another night for the poltergeists to play. The contents of medicine cabinets came crashing out, and alarm clocks were sent flying by the unseen demons. At breakfast, the Russian staff put soaking wet tablecloths on the tables so that the toast racks and condiments could enjoy better purchase. The weather usually settled down in the mornings, but on this occasion the wind was editing our existence while the horizon swung alarmingly, first this way, then that. Five of us – three women and two men – were doing traditional and aerobic exercises up top. I am so clumsy at the best of times that in strolling the main deck I would occasionally trip over a coaming, the steel lip that runs round a hatch. I was in mid-exercise when a freak movement of the ship threw me flat on my back. No damage was done, though Mrs. Murphy, an onlooker, pointed out that I could have fallen on my head "and suffered a repercussion."

Our regular morning exercises were under the baton of Tim, who was after all a former chief petty officer and also one of the fittest-looking people his age I've ever seen. The activity came about in response to a perceived need for some kind of vigorous workout. From the outset, I ate only two meals a day, one of them a breakfast of fruit, toast, and coffee, but I found that my weight remained stable, which disappointed me a bit. So I asked Tim if he would let me join him in his morning regimen. The class kept growing, despite certain drawbacks – particularly the wind, which was merciless. Wind is measured on the Beaufort scale, developed by Admiral Sir Francis Beaufort, RN, in 1806. Zero on the Beaufort scale is a perfectly calm sea, Force 9 is a gale, and Force 12 is a hurricane. The scale goes as high as Force 17, which I don't care to contemplate. That particular workout was conducted in wind so strong that standing upright sometimes proved difficult.

I had read many books preparing for this voyage. One of the most informative was _South Sea Journey_, a 1976 narrative by my friend, the late George Woodcock. Earlier in the 1970s he travelled across a broad sampling of the islands of Polynesia, Melanesia, and Micronesia, studying the effects of independence, a state many of the places had achieved only recently and others were expecting soon. George was born in 1912, meaning that he was eighteen in 1930, when the British Empire reached its numerical zenith. He was of the generation that despised British imperialism as an open sore on society. At the same time, however, such people owed it a great deal. In simple terms, the Empire brought the world to the attention of people like Woodcock and made the whole planet a fit subject for their curiosity. In the end, George, a man of letters and critic, published considerably more than a hundred books. He was also a philosophical anarchist, and thus believed in a society based on a maximum of individual liberty and a minimum of government. In fact, George was the most widely read anarchist writer since Peter Kropotkin (1842–1921), the Russian prince now recognized as the most cogent and systematic anti-authoritarian thinker of the nineteenth century. Kropotkin was trained in science, and his best-known book is _Mutual Aid_, an important gloss on Charles Darwin. It argues that it's the species that cooperate that survive, not the ones that compete.

What did this have to do with our voyage? A good deal actually. In his transition from scientist to social scientist,

Kropotkin perfected his vision of the ideal anarchist society, one in which people go about their tasks with good-natured efficiency and dedication, settle their disputes by organic arbitration rather than by violence, and choose their leaders solely on the basis of ability and experience. George, it seems to me, was always searching for this elusive proto-democratic paradise wherever he travelled (India, East Asia, Latin America) and indeed whenever he travelled in history as well. *South Sea Journey* is even more interesting now than when he wrote it, because it came at a time when many tribal and aboriginal customs, which reflected the Kropotkinesque ideal, were still being practised in the area. More than twenty years later I was expecting to see such characteristics much less in evidence. I was also keeping a sharp eye out for the last vestiges of direct European colonialism in the western Pacific, as well as for the newer proxy imperialism by which some of the former colonial states, such as Australia and New Zealand, currently substitute for their predecessors. Thinking about George Woodcock also made me consider the ship as a little social experiment.

There we were, forty or so people, separated from one another in a number of ways. First, there were lines of authority. The captain ate alone or with the chief engineer to talk ship's business. Not that he was from the upper middle classes; his accent proved otherwise. But when you're the captain you can't be buddies with the people for whose lives you're responsible. Similarly, the other officers did not socialize with the crew. We passengers saw a bit of officers and crew alike, though we could not break down the obvious barriers between the English-speakers and the

Russian-speakers. We couldn't even get along among ourselves. Any mention of nationality, religion, culture in the
broadest sense, or even climate, raised hackles. During one
breakfast, for example, one of the British passengers called
someone else "a typically stupid American tourist" to her
face. Still, I did manage to get us all together on the question
of gratuities. I also considered the morning exercise idea a
success. But most of the time, mutual aid was difficult to
envision, much less achieve.

Once the only clothes dryer on the ship had been fixed
it was literally operating night and day. In fact, the demand
for it appeared to rise as the voyage progressed. Because
there were two washers, everyone was forever complaining about the queues – and this was also why the dryer
seemed to be constantly breaking down. I suggested dividing up the week into fourteen half-days and assigning
everyone a laundry slot of his or her choice, insofar as
possible, but for some reason this was out of the question,
an affront to wounded individualism. Yet the same people
came together, spontaneously and virtually without discussion, to organize an anchor pool – a lottery with sixty
squares at five dollars a square, representing the minutes in
an hour; if the ship were to drop the hook next time at, say,
6:17 or 9:28 (information that was scrupulously recorded
in the ship's log), then the person owning square 17 or
square 28 collected $300.

Being on such a ship is like hanging out in an airport, in
that I defy anyone to do it for more than a few hours and
come away with the notion that democracy works as well
as we like to believe it does. In any case, it occurred to me,
as I took the measure of the voyage thus far, that we

passengers were both natives and colonizers. Natives in the eyes of the English officers, but imperialists in the eyes of the Russian-speaking crew and service staff, who saw only our camcorders and U.S. dollars and ignorant western highjinks. European-style colonialism was always a ship-borne disease, like cholera. Even today there are still faint traces of this unhappy fact.

4

POLYNESIA

*S*OMEWHERE OFF to starboard, not actually in sight but not awfully far away, were the desolate Marquesas Islands, northeast of Tahiti. It was in the Marquesas, in 1841, that Herman Melville jumped ship and lived among cannibals, as he recounted in *Typee*. The book was the only commercial success of Melville's literary career (*Moby-Dick*, his most famous work, was a failure). *Typee* had another distinction as well. It created, or at least made permanent, the public's titillated curiosity about South Pacific cannibals. Human flesh, which I am reliably informed tastes nothing whatever like chicken, was indeed partaken of among native cultures in the region, usually for ritual purposes, though sometimes to reduce the population to sustainable levels. (The ratio of people to resources remains the chief problem in most South Pacific islands today.) And, yes, there were cases of locals consuming the bodies of missionaries. Had there not been such instances, or desert islands with only a single coconut palm, cartoonists would have to fall back on wit to earn a living.

Such images are an embarrassment to South Pacific life today, all the more so because the American and European missionaries continued to come and continue yet. The Gospel-propagators literally could not be eaten fast enough to discourage the evangelical movement that has flourished in the western Pacific for at least a century and a half. This is probably one of the most Christianized parts of the world. It is also a truly enormous area, a third of the globe. In size rather than density, it represents Earth's largest single telephone area-code. (The code, should you wish to call, is 872: satellite connection only, of course.)

Pacific islanders were attacked, dehumanized, at any events wildly romanticized, by whites from the moment the two opposites first came into contact in the sixteenth century. Melville, like Paul Gauguin and Robert Louis Stevenson, or even James A. Michener after them, helped to popularize the notion of a Pacific paradise of gentle breezes, swaying fronds, and gorgeous sunsets. Even if the interpretation was sometimes not implied, it could almost always be inferred. In *Typee*, Melville describes one of the anchorages in the Marquesas this way:

> Deterred by the frightful stories related by its inhabitants, ships never enter this bay.... At long intervals, however, some intrepid captain will touch on the skirts of the bay [for provisions], with two or three armed boats' crews, and accompanied by an interpreter. The natives who live near the sea descry the strangers long before they reach their waters, and aware of the purpose for which they come, pro-claim loudly the news of the approach. By a species of vocal telegraph the intelligence reaches the inmost recesses of the vale in an inconceivably short space of time, drawing the whole population down to the beach laden with every

variety of fruit. The interpreter... leaps ashore with the goods intended for barter, while the boats, with their oars shipped, and every man on his thwart, lie just outside the surf, heading off from shore, in readiness at the first untoward event to escape to the open sea. As soon as the traffic is concluded, one of the boats pulls in under cover of the muskets of the others, the fruit is quickly thrown into her, and the transient visitors precipitately retire from what they justly consider so dangerous a vicinity.

For by the time Melville arrived, centuries of hostility were already on record throughout the Pacific world.

In contrast to North America, to which Europeans came seeking gold and an opening to China, the lure of the Pacific was spices, all manner of spices, used of course to flavour and preserve food, but also to embalm the dead. I had recently re-read Joseph Conrad's novel *Lord Jim*, in anticipation of its centenary, and had come upon this description by Marlow, the narrator, of Patusan, the fictional setting of the story:

> You will find the name of the country pretty often in collections of old voyages. The seventeenth-century traders went there for pepper, because the passion for pepper seemed to burn like a flame of Love in the breast of Dutch and English adventurers about the time of James the First. Where wouldn't they go for pepper? For a bag of pepper they would cut each other's throats without hesitation, and would forswear their soul, of which they were so careful otherwise: the bizarre obstinancy of that desire made them defy death in a thousand shapes; the unknown seas, the loathsome and strange diseases; wounds, captivity, hunger, pestilence, and despair. It made them great! By heavens! it made them heroic; and it made them pathetic, too, in their craving for trade with the inflexible death levying its toll on young and old....

As always, Conrad's prose seems to us a little creaky, with some basso grunts, as well as some of the high-pitched keening that ships seem to emit in the middle of the night; but he knew the various types of colonial mentality, probably would have delighted in the fact that, among the older generation in the Netherlands today, you still sometimes hear the phrase "as expensive as a pound of pepper."

By the 1520s, the Spanish, who were the first to secure a significant foothold in the New World, were regularly shipping huge quantities of silver back to Europe from a base in Panama. Their ships often fell victim to pirates and privateers – often, but not always, French ones. In 1573, England's Sir Francis Drake, the dreaded *El Draque* of the Spanish imagination, actually attacked Panama and sacked it. But the campaign came at the end of one era and the beginning of another – the exploration of the Pacific.

In the 1550s, the Spaniards began trying to avoid the pirates by taking a far longer route back to Europe: the Strait of Magellan at the tip of South America. This fundamental change of policy led to a wave of Pacific mapping and exploration by all the interested parties. Competition for knowledge was fierce. Spanish navigators figured out how to sail back and forth across the Pacific, taking advantage of the easterlies below the Equator (the same route our ship, in fact, followed), but going to the higher latitudes to catch the westerlies for the return to the Americas. By the 1560s, the Portuguese, another traditional enemy of the Spanish, had penetrated the Philippines. Both countries coveted the Moluccas (the Spice Islands of old maps) as a possible stepping-stone to trade with China.

In this atmosphere of discovery, Europeans became obsessed with something else besides spices and specie. They became obsessed with finding what the chart-makers labelled *Terra Australis Incognita*, a place, people became convinced, that was abundant in gold and other riches. There was no evidence for this assumption, but the fever rose and the race was on. In their quest, some people achieved extraordinary feats of navigation. In his own search for spices and *Terra Australis*, Drake went up the Pacific coast of America as far north as the forty-eighth parallel, then south again, stopping in what is now San Francisco Bay, where he heard enticing rumours of gold. He crossed the Pacific to the Indian Ocean, rounded the Cape of Good Hope, then steered north for England. This was in 1579, sixty years after Ferdinand Magellan (1480–1521), the first circumnavigator. Each such venture influenced the next. In the following decade, Thomas Cavendish (1555–92), a protégé of Sir Walter Ralegh, led a large expedition to the Pacific in direct emulation of Drake. Of course, what such people sought was mainly illusory or far distant in time. Australia, when discovered, did not prove to be the counting-house that people had supposed; the spice trade slackened as other sources of the stuff were found; and gold would not be mined in California for another three hundred years. Today, the whole age of Pacific exploration – centuries, really – seems impossibly remote. The reminders one is left with are individual specks on the map, or groups of islands such as the Marquesas, still under French control, while near neighbours (proximity in the Pacific is counted in the thousands of miles) are heavily influenced by the British or their cousins, the Australians and New Zealanders. By contrast,

U.S. power, whether direct or indirect, becomes greater the farther one moves above the Equator, especially now that America has been forced to give up its military and naval facilities in the Philippines.

What you see below the dotted line, however, are the faint traces of the seventeenth- and eighteenth-century concept of mercantilism, a creed rooted in the understanding that two-way trade could never be advantageous to both parties equally, that every transaction produced a winner and a loser. Trade was a war of wits, in which one attempted to be self-sufficient, importing as little as possible, exporting as much as one could get away with. In its pure form, the concept was lost with the dismantling of the big colonial empires after the Second World War. In those days, culture, or the best of it, tended to move pretty freely from place to place, but not goods. Now goods go freely, but not cultures. These days the people of the world aren't looking for opium or ginseng or tea or beaver pelts for hats, as of old. Certainly the developed world is not crying out for coconut products, which makes the voyages of the *Pride of Great Yarmouth* so charmingly anachronistic. These days the whole world wants the same things. It's now simply a question of who can make them most cheaply. It's now a matter of American popular culture and Japanese electronics for delivery: software and hardware. The concept of comity – the friendly respect for other nations' laws and cultures – has been lost. Our Tahitian destination promised to be so interesting because in no other place has the loss been so obvious for so long, or recognized as such a symbol. In the eighteenth century, when the British and the French stumbled on it almost simultaneously, Tahiti instantly became a kind of shorthand for the concept of a *paradiso terrestre*. But almost from the start it was a paradise lost, or rather a paradise bungled.

In 1767, Philip Carteret, the British explorer with the French name, happened on Tahiti, hoping he had discovered the reclusive Australia. He found the Polynesians physically beautiful and of peaceful demeanour. The following year, the Frenchman Louis Antoine de Bougainville (1729–1811) put in there, too, during his circumnavigation of the world. He thought the Polynesians fascinating, with their animist beliefs and their tattooing, their clan structure, their boat-building and sailing skills. Not that he was blind to what, to his European eyes, was their barbarous side: for example, the custom of infanticide when the population grew too large.

James Cook, Joseph Banks, Samuel Wallis, and of course William Bligh were some of the other early names associated with Tahiti, a place that became quite a vogue in Europe, a subject of fancy and a topic of intellectual fashion. As early as the 1770s (when Tahitians had already been introduced to European tools, weapons, and venereal disease, and were intermarrying with whites), "Tahiti" – the quotation marks are necessary to distinguish the concept from the geographical reality – was all the rage in London salons. The Polynesians were seen not exactly as noble savages, but rather as residents of Eden and without vice. In Paris, it was the same. One of Bougainville's men wrote in the *Mercure de France* that the Tahitian "knows only one God, the God of Love." Bougainville called Tahiti by the name New Cythera (after the birthplace of Venus). Diderot, the encyclopaedist, urged him to leave the spot alone.

Cook was of course a tremendous sailor and explorer, but was perceived as a dull personality, who, given half a chance, would write like the mathematician and astronomer that he was – as indeed his published journals prove. Accordingly, the assignment to produce a ripping narrative of his adventures was doled out to one of the literary johnnies who are forever to be found on the fringes of court, partially obscured by the luxuriant draperies. Dr. John Hawkesworth thus became Cook's ghostwriter. He had a lively style but suffered savage handicaps. He had not been along on Cook's expeditions. In fact, he had never been to sea, and didn't seem to understand what all the different ropes were for. For one reason and another, then, Dr. Hawkesworth laid on the paradise stuff pretty thick, attracting mockery from Samuel Johnson and Horace Walpole. Bougainville had enticed (or kidnapped) a young Tahitian named Ahu-Turu back to Paris. The poor Polynesian became the darling of the intellectuals, a kind of mascot. The British had one of their own, called Oma, who was granted an audience by George III and painted by Sir Joshua Reynolds. In time, he became an actor, playing himself on stage.

∿

Sparks and I were leaning over the ship's rail, talking like two guys standing at a bar. As we watched the flying fish at work below us, Sparks imparted more of his ship-knowledge. "This has got to be the craziest vessel in the Pacific," he said. "Built for use in the Arctic, of all places. Totally unsuited to these conditions. Doesn't have a bilge

keel." He was referring to the steel rim below the waterline
of a heavily laden vessel: the thing that gives the ship a
waistline, so to speak, thus increasing stability. "This hull's
like a log with one side planed off for a deck. So it rolls like
a log too. You're from Canada, you should know what I'm
talking about when I say 'Great Lakes ore carrier.' "

I said indeed I did.

"I sailed on one of them once that had been modified,
supposedly, as a deep-water vessel. It was worse than being
on a destroyer in the navy. Well, this rolls worse than *that*."

Shortly after these words were uttered, at about 0930 on
our twenty-ninth day at sea, we sighted land. The volcanic
peaks of Tahiti, both the main island and its small sister,
Mooréa, loomed in the distance, maybe 48 kilometres (30
miles) away, not vivid green, as they would be when we got
closer, but rather faint black silhouettes, like weak images
produced by an almost-dry rubber stamp. For the next
couple of hours, all the passengers were up on deck, passing
around binoculars and excitedly making plans. In 1891
(pre–Panama Canal days), it took Paul Gauguin more than
twice as long as it took us, sixty-three days to be precise, to
steam from France to Tahiti, a place that, I was surprised
to learn, is a perfectly decent *port autonome,* or container
terminal, but not a particularly desirable anchorage.

The harbour of Papeete, the capital, didn't impress me as
being one of great natural beauty in its own right, such
as San Francisco's or Sydney's, though the water looked like
sparkling mouthwash. More striking were the lush ridge-
backed mountains, which run almost to the shore, leaving
only a small shelf for Papeete (pronounced Pa–pay–EH–tay,
except by some of the British, who contemptuously call it

Paw-PETE). The community is far more cosmopolitan than its relatively small population, about 140,000, would suggest, and is not architecturally unattractive, though hardly any buildings predate the Great Fire of 1884 and most of the big hotels and shopping complexes are from the 1960s, 1970s, and 1980s. When we passed the seawall, we found the harbour full of mysterious-looking small coastal freighters, including a Chinese one with laundry drying in the rigging, and the usual tuna boats and fancy yachts. Tied up opposite the tourist bureau was the P&O cruise ship *Star Princess* (nine decks and, I would guess, 1,200 or 1,300 passengers). The cargo operations of the famous and wonderfully named Peninsular & Oriental Steam Navigation Company are now Dutch-owned, but the liners are still British, though this one at least is of Panamanian registry. When we laid eyes on this palatial gleaming white ship we knew instantly what its presence meant: the city would be full of British and American holiday-makers, and although it was a Monday the shops and nightclubs and the foreigners-only casinos would be doing a roaring trade.

A stream of officials came aboard. First was the harbour-master. Next came the agent, who carried a sack of mail for passengers and crew and also a cellphone, so that those wanting to get into town could call taxis to meet them at the security gate. Finally, there was Tahiti's chief stevedore, who enjoyed a local monopoly. We were the only big freighter in port at the time, leaving two empty berths at the Overseas Wharf, directly opposite the Cruiseship Wharf where the *Star Princess* lay. But there were all these coastal and inter-island vessels tied up, and the stevedoring outfit had only so many crews. How should the boss divide his labour force?

Work at the *Pride of Great Yarmouth* until the job was done, running his men at double pay some of the time? Or spread the work more evenly, so that a few men worked each vessel simultaneously? This was the subject of intensive and very private bargaining between our master and the chief stevedore. Such negotiations always appeared to be in the latter's favour, for in fact he ended up working his people day and night, unloading our cargo using our own cranes, and still managed to take nearly three entire days doing so.

Our carrying capacity, or deadweight tonnage, was almost 17,000 tonnes. We left France with about 13,000 tonnes. Almost half of that cargo, namely 6,000 tonnes, was destined for Papeete. First off the ship, by way of the drawbridge-like ramp that folds out onto the wharf, was the ro-ro cargo, including a few Peugeot automobiles. Personally, I felt some guilt on this score: the last thing they needed in Papeete, with its heavy traffic and heavier pollution, was more cars. Meanwhile, the pot-bellied Tahitian dockers climbed up into the cabs of the ship's four big Swedish-built cranes and began unloading the steel, flour, and other products. This is dangerous work, and it seemed to me miraculous that none of the people down in Number Three hold was crushed by the huge steel slabs swinging wildly back and forth from a great hook. As it was, two bulkhead panels came crashing down after the crane bumped them, and a welder had to be summoned to re-affix them, a task that took several hours. Gantries on the pier were also in operation, whittling down the stacks of containers on deck.

A few of these receptacles cleared French customs with surprising speed. As I left the ship for the forty-five-minute trip round the harbour and into town, I saw one of the excited consignees waving about his bills of lading and searching for the right key with which to open a particular container. I lingered in the shade, curious to see what lay inside. The container was one of the large-size ones. When the doors swung open, it proved to be packed full of what looked like used clothing in clear plastic bags 1.5 metres (5 feet) high. At about noon, I used the first overseas telephone I found to call my wife in Toronto, where, I figured, it was 7 a.m. (though I wasn't positive which day). I woke her from a sound sleep. Even taking that fact into account, I couldn't tell whether she was still being distant with me over my long absence or whether the connection was poor. I hoped for the best.

In preparation for going ashore, I had made and kept an appointment with Serge, one of the Russian oilers down in the engine room, who practises both barbering and women's hairstyling on the side to earn a few extra bucks. Besides a fresh haircut, I was wearing olive-green fatigues that I had washed and pressed the night before. I must have been looking even more spruce than I fancied, because when I passed a French guard in his glass booth he gave me a crisp salute. I returned it with what I hoped was convincing negligence, with a bit of a snap at the very end.

Most of the other passengers went over to Mooréa, 17 kilometres (11 miles) west, by catamaran, which is twice as fast as the car ferry. I set out to explore Papeete and complete a list of chores there. I needed to replenish some basic supplies, mundane items like Plax and toothpaste, and to buy New Zealand dollars, since Auckland was our next stop and I tried to stay one country ahead in my currency dealings. I discovered that no one charges a commission to exchange French francs, of which I still had a few, into so-called Pacific francs. This is one of the subtle benefits enjoyed by French expats, who may live and work in Tahiti indefinitely, whereas other citizens of the European Union may remain only three years. There are many such perks.

The French speak of *le mirage*, the illusion that Tahiti is a tropical paradise, remote from the worries of the world, full of beautiful bodies on topless beaches and the air heavy with the scent of flowers everywhere. Maintenance of *le mirage* is essential to the tourist economy, and keeping up appearances is easy enough, given what remains of the splendid remoteness of the place. As I walked up the rue Paul Gauguin (he was an outcast when he lived here, but now a street and a school are named for him, and reproductions of his work are everywhere), the following thought struck me. Gauguin has been falsely praised by urban critics for the genius with which, in his Polynesian pictures, he used little patches of ground as part of the composition, as a watercolourist would do. Of course he kept the paint thin so that the canvas sometimes showed through. My God, he was 16,000 kilometres (10,000 miles) from Loomis & Tooles or Winsor & Newton, or whoever supplied his materials; he could hardly afford to squander pigment. He obviously had a reliable source of canvas, though. Still, he sometimes painted on wood or even glass. It was a Gauguin painting-on-glass that Somerset Maugham salvaged when he visited Tahiti during the First World War, a dozen years after Gauguin's lonely death on one of the islands in the Marquesas group, from syphilis, aged fifty-five. The Gauguin museum on Tahiti has none of his paintings, just as Cézanne's atelier in Aix-en-Provence has no Cézannes.

The Gauguin museum does own some of Gaugin's wood-block prints, however, which are almost as interesting as his wood sculptures.

I wandered to the Marché. Every populated South Pacific island, it seems, has such an open-sided market building for local produce and handicrafts. This one was especially large (two big storeys) and well-stocked, selling everything from fresh pork to life-sized penises carved out of sandalwood. While there, I ran into the ship's purser, along with the agent. The purser explained that, though he didn't usually take on any stores in Tahiti, because of high prices, he was nonetheless breaking down this time and getting enough fresh produce to see us through to Auckland, where everything is much cheaper. This was indeed good news. After a month at sea our salads had become pretty flimsy, and the vegetables in general had taken on that floating-in-formaldehyde look. Around the Marché, and also around the tiny cathedral, a couple of blocks to the south and east, the area was lively and bohemian in character. Numerous Chinese shops tried to sell everything imaginable from one room, in the manner of Chinese shops round the world, and there were also some examples of the *club privé* and some interesting restaurants. These ranged from Chinese ("chao-men 500F") to, of course, Polynesian (serving *poisson cru*, the national dish – raw fish marinated in lemon juice and coconut milk). Other eating-places catered to the overseas French. I may be accused of bias in the matter, but it's always seemed to me that, whenever the French have colonized a place, they leave behind a legacy of cruelty and rich sauces, whereas the British leave behind condescension, parliamentary government, and public libraries.

I don't mean that to sound flippant. Tahiti, I believe, might profitably be compared to Bermuda, a British colony of some beauty (if Atlantic beauty), where only permanent residents are permitted to drive automobiles and great effort goes into building the infrastructure as well as protecting the environment, both natural and architectural. Tahiti has efficient and inexpensive public transport, not just frequent inter-island ferries but also the institution known as *le truck*, a large van or ute, but with length-wise wooden benches; by this method one can travel almost anywhere on the main islands for the equivalent of a dollar-fifty. Significantly, though, Tahiti lacks a modern waste-disposal system. Even the sewage from the big hotels is pumped into the ocean. Also, the French make an ostentatious display of their military presence here. Aside from a tank farm, the most prominent harbour facility is a French naval base, with large buildings hidden behind walls topped with razor wire. The day we arrived, a destroyer escort was tied up there. Next to it was a sort of landing tender, quite large; this is the naval equivalent of a ro-ro, with a hinged stern that opens outward so that the area between hulls can be flooded and landing craft floated out, as one would do in an amphibious assault. Various more ominous French warships patrol these waters. The practice has been going on for more than 150 years. This combination of disregard for the environment and obsession with military might, far beyond that characteristic of contemporary Britain, found its most notorious expression in the French policy of above-ground nuclear testing in the Pacific. This course of action seems to have changed Tahiti forever from a dégagé place to one that is very engagé indeed.

Open-air testing of the atomic bomb, like the bomb
itself, was an American innovation. In 1954, the United
States upped the stakes by testing the first deliverable hydro-
gen bomb on the Bikini atoll in the Pacific. In 1963, France
detonated its first H-bomb on the Mururoa atoll in French
Polynesia. More than twenty years later, through successive
governments, the French tests continued at irregular intervals. Protests grew, in France and elsewhere, but had little
practical effect. Such was the nature of European colonialism that, even in the post-colonial era, the French totally
dominated its Pacific islands without allowing them a voice
in French affairs. Even now, whereas French colonies in the
Caribbean and the Indian Ocean are *départements*, French
Polynesia comes under the heading of *territoires outre-mer*.

The controversy seemed to reach a crescendo in 1985
when Greenpeace was poised to send a converted trawler,
the *Rainbow Warrior*, into the Mururoa testing area to
disrupt a particularly important blast. Before the environ-
mentalist group could do so, however, agents of the French
secret service, the Direction générale des services extérieurs,
destroyed the ship in Auckland Harbour, killing one crew
member. An international incident ensued. The DGSE and
other intelligence agencies are said to be active in Tahiti,
where their members like to dine in the seventh-floor
restaurant of the Hôtel Kon Tiki Pacific in Papeete, a
hostelry also favoured by the French military, of whom
there are many to be seen; they're part of the permanent
garrison in French Polynesia, most of it based at the
Quartier Boche barracks in the avenue Bruat. One might
even see members of the Foreign Legion, with their white
kepis and paratrooper boots, for there are still 8,500 officers

and men in the Legion, most either seconded to the UN or found among the 5,000 French troops still making trouble in Africa (where France has intervened militarily twenty times since the 1960s).

In the past, the Legion could not legally have French non-commissioned officers, but of course it did and does, all its former Nazis having died off by now. Nor is it supposed to fight in France itself, though it received dispensation to do so in both world wars. I was fascinated to have pointed out to me one of the former legionnaires who had retired in Tahiti. On enlistment, recruits are given new identities (and this in France, where changing one's name legally, in civil court, is almost impossible); after five years' service they are granted French citizenship. The Legion is a sort of Frankenstein's monster, a rogue element in the military, too dangerous to keep alive but too useful to politicians to kill off – and too handy for implementing less-than-public policy. In the 1960s, remember, Legion officers were forever plotting to kill President de Gaulle. How dangerous will such people be when there is no longer a colony to which they can be sent?

For, to be sure, French Polynesia has been becoming more independence-minded, especially since September 1995, when the French president of the time, Jacques Chirac, lifted a three-year ban on new nuclear tests. This caused large-scale anti-government riots in Papeete. As it happened, the *Pride of Great Yarmouth* had been making its first visit to the port at that time, and it had to retreat to open water to avoid becoming a possible victim of mistaken identity, as mobs took to burning buildings in the centre of the city. France's new socialist PM, Lionel Jospin, has begun cutting back on the military overseas (and at home). Will he continue? François Mitterrand was a socialist as well, and he did little or nothing in this regard. What seems clear to me after talking to Tahitians in Papeete is that the French, singly and en masse, are disliked, and perhaps, on balance, even hated. This island is one of the few places in the world where Europeans are viewed in much friendlier fashion once they are overheard speaking English, German, or Italian – anything but French.

Speaking of matters military, I am one of those old-fashioned travellers – perhaps even the last of the breed – who, on arriving in a new place, likes to inspect the fortifications. Keeping defences in good repair is an important measure of civic culture, like having an efficient postal system. For example, a friend in Boston, when I first visited there for any length of time, asked what I wanted to do. I said I wished to take the National Park Service landing craft to a remote island in the harbour to see the Civil War–era fortress. Being a good sport, my host obliged. Now, on my second day in Tahiti, I was seized with the notion of locating the nineteenth-century French fort that is reported to exist at the head of the Fautaua Valley. This proved to be a wild goose chase, but it succeeded in getting me out of Papeete and into the countryside for a look-see.

Only one of the several guidebooks at our disposal mentioned the site, and it provided no details and gave what turned out to be overly confusing directions. I was ready to go at dawn, with a litre of water and a bottle of number 45 sunblock. The city was very quiet, perhaps hung over from a rough night of prayer and fasting, but the market was beginning to stir, and I paused to buy a pineapple from a grower unloading his van at one of the stalls. I began traipsing due south, away from the harbour, and in half an hour had crossed the city and come to a blue-collar residential area where the small lime-coated houses were surrounded by crude walls topped with broken glass. Everyone thereabouts had a guard dog, and the dogs carried word of my approach by the canine telegraph. Soon some pretty fierce beasts were straining at their enclosures as I passed, craving a piece of me. I addressed them individually, using the familiar *tu* form, but this did no good. After three-quarters of an hour, this section petered out and was replaced by rural shantytowns and the sound of roosters crowing. One no-doubt-prominent family owned a billy goat. He was tethered in their front yard and looked remarkably like the late Ho Chi Minh.

There was a river to my left. In higher latitudes it would be called a stream or a creek, though I daresay it surges during the rainy season, which would not begin here for another month or two. As I followed the river towards its source, heading further into the interior, the elevation rose quickly from near-sea-level to, I would guess, 1,000 metres (3,300 feet). Habitations were few at this point and vegetation more tropical, with enormous groves of bamboo in the lowest-lying areas and ferny rain forest everywhere else. A few steps from the bitumen road the terrain became impassable, as much because of volcanic boulders as because of vines and tangled undergrowth.

The paved road, such as it was, gave out at Bain Loti, a place so named because it is the setting of *Raruhu* (1880), the first novel by the French writer Louis-Marie Julien Viaud, who used the pen-name Pierre Loti (and later retitled the work *The Marriage of Loti*). This wide spot in the bush is the place where *le truck* turns around and returns to civilization, and it is graced with a fey-looking bust of Loti with his hands crossed over his sternum. It had taken me more than two hours to get there on foot from the wharf, so, despite heavy smoke from a brush fire, I decided to pause here and eat my lunch. For this purpose I had brought along a kitchen knife from the ship's galley. I was glad that I was using it to anatomize my pineapple rather than to defend myself from a pack of feral dogs, as I had feared at one point. The water around me appeared swift but not deep. Another trekker, who apparently had worked up an appetite equal to my own, had waded across the rippling shallows and was building a cook-fire on the opposite bank. High above her, laid into the steep side of the mountain, were two flights of crumbling stone steps, leading nowhere.

Beyond this point I began to get lost. The guidebook indicated that one must follow the dirt road starting at Bain Loti and cross a wooden footbridge. In fact, there were two dirt roads, neither marked, heading in the same general direction. Within the space of a few kilometres, I encountered three wooden footbridges, one of them with planks so rotten that I wouldn't want to risk crossing it a second time. Now and then I passed a Tahitian resident, usually a woman in a brightly coloured *pareu*. I always tipped my hat, smiled, and emitted a cheery bonjour. Some people responded in kind, others pointedly ignored me. I had the sense that those who snubbed me were under the impression that I was from France. There were also one or two micro-businesses which appeared before the unpaved road turned into a trail and then a path. One was a Chinese shop, another a garage. At both I stopped, tried to chat, and asked directions to the fort, spreading out my map. At each place I witnessed the same scene. A woman admitted she'd never heard of an old French fort in these parts but examined my map and showed me where I was and which way I should proceed to get to the Fautaua Falls (which at some points I fancied I could hear rumbling in the distance). Then the man of the place would strut over, speak sharply to the helpful woman, grab the map from my hand, and turn it sideways and upside down and begin pointing knowingly to all manner of faraway destinations, speaking very quickly in the local language. I resolved never to ask a man for directions if there were a woman to ask instead.

I walked for another hour and was surprised to find a low-lying prefab building in the valley. This turned out to be the home of the water-management officers who monitor the volume and purity of the river, which supplies drinking water to Papeete. A French office worker was the only person about. She was surprised to see me. She, too, knew nothing of the existence of any old French fort except that one needed a permit from the Hôtel de Ville to go there. The fallacious logic was more than I could cope with in French. Instead, I thanked her and continued on.

One difficulty in my not being able to find the damned fort was that I didn't have a proper topographical map. More important, I couldn't imagine what it was the French thought they were protecting. A work built way up there would have had no bearing at all on Papeete harbour. There would have been shore batteries for that. Even a superficial examination of the city's grid shows what the situation must

have been, with defences all along the first significant
elevation behind the port, which is still, tellingly so, called
the rue des Remparts. The Fautaua Valley runs only about
a third of the way across the island, and the crests on either
side are not even the highest spots. Therefore a fort here
would have been no prophylaxis against a landing on the far
side of the island, either. In any event, the opposite side is
shielded by treacherous reefs. No, the place that wanted
defending was the narrow isthmus between the main
portion of the island and the peninsular section called Tahiti
Iti. One set of defences there would have prevented an
invasion threat from the north or the south. Building near
the Fautaua Falls would have had less obvious benefit and
would have been an engineering nightmare and, once
building was completed, it would have been almost impossible to keep supplied. At the end of the twentieth century,
I could scarcely get through this countryside at all. What
must the interior have been like in the nineteenth?

The landscape, though, was beautiful. When I was high
enough I saw wild orchids, for example. But the sun was
punitive, absolutely brutal. I got along a bit farther and saw
a fellow bushwalker at a clearing in the distance. He was a
German about my age, killing time for a couple of days
before taking deck passage to the Marquesas on a German
ship. He had actually been to the place that I sought and was
now making his descent back into town. He had come out
with no sunscreen, so I gave him some of mine. He told me
that he was turned back a few kilometres from where we
were on the grounds that he had violated a *zone militaire*.
He seemed surprised that I hadn't been chased out as well.

We sat on a fallen tree, resting, sweat cascading down our faces, arms, and backs. "If the fort exists, it's up there some- where," he said, pointing to the nearby vertical face of the mountain, an endless mat of dense growth atop black rock. "A climber would need ten litres of water to get there in this heat," he reasoned, "and that is probably more than one would be able to carry." We remained chatting in the shade until our hearts resumed their normal rhythms.

I returned to Papeete the way I had come, which as far as I could determine was the only route. When I got to the city, I caught a view of myself in a mirror-like shop window. I was filthy, and my clothes were tattered and torn, so I cleaned myself up as best I could in the lavatory of a coffee bar. I had been hiking a full day. My ageing feet had almost ceased functioning.

Tired and dishevelled as I was, I was tempted into a wine merchant's in the high street. As Tahiti is a duty-free port, prices are more or less the same as on the ship, but the variety is of course far better, as ships have a propensity for plonk. I spent some time looking about and finally, con- templating the two and a half months still to go, bought a case of decent Chardonnay. I explained to the shopkeeper that, because I was travelling without a servant, I wondered whether he employed a lad who could deliver my purchase to the freighter *Pride of Great Yarmouth* berthed at the Over- seas Wharf. Indeed he did, he said, carefully writing down the ship's name. As I left, in the process causing a little bell above the door to tinkle, he said something else. He spoke quickly, so I couldn't quite catch the words. I believe what he said was to the effect of "It is a pleasure to serve a visitor who appreciates the old ways."

Back aboard the ship that night, sitting in my cabin with the steel door open, soaking my feet, I saw Tim Beneke. He had just returned from his own *eleven-hour* hike across the razor-backed ridges of the Fautaua. Part of the way he had had to move hand-over-hand from one exposed root to another. He said a local resident told him that in fact nothing at all remains of the fort, whatever it was, except the broken stairs near Bain Loti that I had seen, while missing their significance.

"Whatever it might have been at one time," Tim said, speaking like the former career officer that he was, "I don't think it was a posting that men vied for. I don't claim to know anything about the French military, but I'd guess that this was one of those places you were ordered to when you screwed up big time."

We shared a bottle of my wine, which was by then nicely chilled.

5

SHIPMATES

*W*HILE WE WERE en route to New Zealand, relations between the British passengers and the American ones deteriorated further. There was no single incident of rudeness or anger, just a general lowering of tone, and increase in volume, to the point that the captain refused to be in the dining room with any of us. After we left, one of the cooks would phone the bridge to say that the coast was clear. Only then did the master come down for his breakfast, lunch, or dinner. I can't say I blamed him.

Discord took a couple of forms. First, the two nationalities generally do despise each other. Virtually any statement that comes out of the mouth of one aggravates the disposition of the other. Second, a long voyage such as this tends to isolate for inspection certain weak spots in people's characters. The retired British doctor, for example, turned out to be a bully, never happier than when he could say or do something to hurt or humiliate another. When we crossed the Equator, he persuaded two of the female passengers that the ritual initiation for first-timers was to let him cut their pubic hair: a tradition of his own devising.

Suddenly, I appreciated the differences between the two American women I had come to think of as New Age and Seagrams. New Age ate everything but porridge and ice cream with her fingers, used *like* and *okay* in every sentence, and was otherwise what the Chinese call a piece of uncut jade, but she was kind-hearted, generous, and cheerful. We all felt sorry for her when she ate an unwashed salad ashore in Papeete and lay sick as a hound for three days, unable to keep down any sustenance. Seagrams was another type entirely. She seldom spoke except at the top of her lungs and was both crude and chauvinistic. I knew we were in for rough seas, socially speaking, when I passed by the open door to her cabin and saw her stapling placemats with patriotic scenes all over the panelled bulkheads. Apparently she couldn't sleep unless surrounded by photographic images of Mount Rushmore, the White House, the Grand Canyon, and so on. "Why can't you people talk like Americans?" she actually said to two of the British women one day. Her favourite rejoinder was "Bullshit!"

She had taken a particular dislike to me, doubtless because to her I seemed British, yet somehow had a North American voice. I was obviously some sort of fifth columnist or agent provocateur. One morning I came down to breakfast to find her leading an argument about whether the thumb counted as a finger. Not a discussion, an argument. Tempers flared. Without the benefit of coffee in my bloodstream, I made the mistake of trying to change the subject to an issue of some immediate benefit or enduring importance – something on a little higher conversational plane at least.

"You!" she hollered at me in a raspy caw. "You go sit over there!"

She pointed to the other table, the one favoured by officers.

I had no intention of arguing with her. As Oscar Wilde said, that would be engaging in a battle of wits with an unarmed opponent. In any case, at that hour I didn't have the patience to explain that etiquette is a division of morality, not the other way around. I meekly removed myself to the other table.

My exile had been going on for several days when we reached either our thirty-sixth or thirty-seventh day at sea, depending on how one deals with the day that disappeared when we crossed the International Date Line. Perhaps the charitable explanation for our behaviour in the dining room was that we were all going a bit troppo, as our Australian friends like to say. The day that vanished on the Date Line, incidentally, was a Monday. Going westward like this, the company gets two days' work out of the crew for a single day's pay. Coming back, captains are careful to regulate a ship's speed so the recrossing won't result in two Saturdays or two Sundays back to back. Otherwise they would be paying *double* time-and-a-half in wages. Wages are the second-largest expense in operating a ship, coming a distant second to fuel, which, with both engines running, we burned at the rate of about sixty-five tonnes a day. Given an average price of US$100 a tonne, that works out to about US$800,000 for each complete circumnavigation. The economic reasoning behind a voyage such as this continues to elude my understanding.

Summer had not yet come to New Zealand, for it was the antipodean equivalent of April 1 there. As we steamed south from Tahiti, the air, wind, and water turned as chilly as human relations in the dining room. It was blanket weather. Much of the time a light rain swept horizontally across the deck. Yet in another sense the weather was gorgeous. In the Pacific, I found, most sunrises are spectacular in the same way, while each sunset is stunning in its own particular manner. Sometimes the clouds acted like venetian blinds, hiding the reddish-orange sun in the west. At other times, clouds ran in both directions, with the crosswise ones seemingly supported by the perpendicular type, which looked like pylons in the sky. Then there were days when the whole scene was billowy, like the sky in some old Italian fresco. For several nights we travelled under a beautiful gibbous moon.

The loutish Tahitian stevedores had left a frightful mess of beer cans and assorted rubbish all up and down the deck. One morning during callisthenics (we wore double sweatshirts for warmth and had to hang on to the rail for stability at times), we observed some crew members clearing up the debris. One of them gathered all the dunnage – broken two-by-fours and splintered pieces of skids mostly – and made it into one gigantic faggot. I had hoped that he was intending to put it in old drums and burn it, so we could warm ourselves. But no, he hauled the wood aloft, swung the bundle over the side, then let it go by cutting the rope with his knife. (The sailors all carried knives.) At least wood will biodegrade. Crew also had been observed furtively tossing plastic bags of garbage and even old paint cans over the taffrail. Such actions violated the industry's own international waste-disposal codes. But Nature has its revenge. Salt water and sea air take a terrible toll on the products of humankind. Radios, tape-recorders, and CD players could barely make it through a voyage like this with their tiny parts intact. Every foot of wire rope and cable had to be given a protective inch or so of heavy grease each time out. In South Pacific conditions, the standard steel shipping container is expected to last only ten years before the bottom rusts out. The very ships themselves have surprisingly short lives, the more recent ones especially. Our old Soviet hull was said to be constructed of steel of such quality and thickness seldom seen in the West and never used nowadays in new vessels. Our captain, according to the gossip I heard, enjoyed an enviable reputation for safety and also for returning with his vessel, whichever one he was commanding, in a state of good repair.

He was also, I observed, a punctual master. To date, all of our arrivals had been on the scheduled day, despite the fact that our departures had all been delayed by the work-to-rule attitudes and other such gamesmanship of dockers at the various ports. We were three days getting unloaded in Tahiti, as I mentioned. While this represented a recreational and gastronomic windfall for us passengers (supernumerary cargo, as we were known officially), it naturally drove the master mad. He was therefore under pressure to make up for lost time in the six-day run to New Zealand. Another reason for his haste, we understood, was that a member of the shipping line's board of directors happened to be in Auckland on business and had expressed a wish to come aboard. We were burning fuel at a furious rate; for two days on the run our speed *averaged* 18.6 knots, which was faster than I thought the vessel could even travel. Mind you, we were moving much lighter in the water after discharging so much in Papeete. The ride was extremely fast, bumpy, and exciting.

The fact that a director was to come aboard might also have been one reason why the captain ordered a clean-up on a scale we hadn't witnessed before. I don't mean to say that crew members were polishing the brightwork. The *Pride of Great Yarmouth* had no such brass fixtures. Seen at medium distance, in fact, it looked a dilapidated old thing, with huge rust patches on the sides that resembled the continents on some imaginary map of the world. But suddenly a tremendous amount of painting was going on. Even the lifeboats were given a new coat of Day-Glo orange. Ship hygiene and upkeep had been falling in priority of late, what with computer and cargo difficulties. In fact, the two sets of problems were tied together inextricably. The ship's computer was refusing to spit out work orders or absorb the records of maintenance jobs completed. So all this information had to be transmitted orally, from one watch to the next, in at least two languages. Inevitably, some tasks were overlooked. The crew had to be ordered to dig in and put matters right. As Mrs. Murphy observed in her inimitable style, "It's time to bite the Bible and get down to business." Sparks, her husband, made the face he usually made at such moments.

We would be losing two familiar figures in New Zealand. Hamish, the Russian-speaking computer geek from somewhere near Dundee, had become too frustrated with the ship's digital backwardness. Despite entreaties from the company, he would be paying out at Auckland and returning to Scotland via Honolulu, Los Angeles, and New York. Molly represented the other departure; she was returning to her native place on the South Island. She would be especially missed for the innocent sincerity with which she said wholly extraordinary things. When the usual cultural and personal tensions had cast a light coating of frost on mealtime, she inevitably came bounding in, late and full of cheer; the first words out of her mouth were always, "So, what's the crack today then?" One night, in talking about her boyfriend, she uttered, in complete earnest, the following sentences: "I don't like the term *partner*. It sounds a wee bit vulgar." She pronounced the word something like Volga, as in Olga from the Volga. "So I jest call him me main *prog*." She went on to reminisce about growing up in a farmhouse where a rooster and a couple of sheep lived in the kitchen. We were all helpless with laughter.

There was a little farewell party for the two of them. Hamish spoke, with the nostalgia of the still-young, about his first ship, a coaster that worked the Irish Sea. "We used to have what we called the bond run," he said. "This involved going more than 30 miles [48 kilometres] out, into international waters, so that we qualified as a vessel in transit and could open the beer and liquor without paying duty on it. We'd be gone a day and a half, using maybe twenty tonnes of fuel at $150 a tonne, so's we could have a drink."

I saw Seagrams standing in the corner sullenly eyeing me. She obviously felt she couldn't let loose and have a good time with me present. So, after wishing the two ship-jumpers safe passage, I had one drink and withdrew early, just as the music was getting loud. I don't know what I missed by doing so, but the crew joined the party in twos and threes every time the watch changed, and in the morning I heard the sweet, solicitous Scotswoman, a former nurse, say to Molly, who was packing: "Now, dear, did you remember to pack your shoes from last night? And your dress? Did you go and retrieve your dress this morning?"

ॐ

New Zealand arrived in the night, like a particularly pleasant dream. I awoke at five in the morning to find that we were already tied up at the Wynard Oil Wharf in Auckland, where we were both discharging soya oil from Europe and taking on additional fuel. I don't pretend to have a finely tuned understanding of how this system works, but we kept bunker oil, the lifeblood of the ship, in four tanks, two port and two starboard, in addition to the main fuel storage area along the keel. There was also a smaller tank in the engine room itself. And sometimes fuel is purchased not to be burned immediately but rather to be used as ballast until needed. Such was the case in this instance, because we would be off-loading five thousand tonnes of cargo in New Zealand, practically emptying the ship before shifting back into French territory.

The *Pride of Great Yarmouth* was scheduled to spend half a day at the oil wharf before crossing the harbour to the Jellicoe Wharf in the general cargo area. There we would not only unload other types of goods but even backload some stuff destined for Espíritu Santo in Vanuatu: an example of the efficient use of port time that makes shipowners feel warm inside. Yet the stevedoring problem at Auckland was the worst of any we had encountered so far. In fairness, the situation could not be laid entirely at the

dockers' door. Bad blood obviously existed between the
stevedores of Auckland and this ship or, more likely, this
company's fleet of ships. The men appeared to work hap-
hazardly for a few moments before breaking for smokes
and stubbies. Our crew did nothing to heal the old wounds,
whatever they were, but engaged in such petty pranks as
hiding the clamps used to secure one container to another.

Watching all the goings-on was an education. At one
point, a small-size container right under my porthole came
open, revealing a consignment of onions in net bags, and also
T-shirts. The consignee of the T-shirts, whoever and wherever he or she might be, would find that the goods had been
slightly short-landed. As the day progressed there was talk of
our actually becoming the target of an official job-action.
I'm not sure why. For part of the afternoon no stevedoring
at all was accomplished, as no stevedores were even in sight.
At the top of the gangway, the bosun and the purser always
set up a chalkboard, telling those with time off the hour at
which they must return (usually sixty minutes before sailing).
In Auckland, the sign read: SHORE LEAVE EXPIRES AT
1600HRS. BE ONBOARD AT 1500HRS SOBER. That last
phrasing was standard. Sometimes it worked, sometimes it
didn't. My own observation on this voyage was that the
chalked notice, overall, could not be taken literally, as
the hour of departure was forever being revised. This was
frustrating for the passengers, who feared that they didn't
have time to venture very far inland, only to learn later that
this hadn't been the case. In Auckland, the time of embarka-
tion was rewritten three times. Finally, after ultimata from
both labour and capital, the ship departed at the close of
business on the third day. The unmistakable sound of one

of the generators firing confirmed the intention to leave, and a moment later, both massive engines came alive again in a teeth-rattling resurrection.

All of which is to say that I got to see more of New Zealand's largest city (with 850,000 of the country's 3.5 million people and few of the far-more-numerous sheep) than I had dared hope. And that I was quite taken with it, as I had expected to be.

I remember that George Woodcock, after his detailed circuit of the South Pacific some twenty-five years ago, came back saying that Auckland in the 1970s reminded him of Toronto in the 1950s. He did not intend this as a compliment. But in fact Auckland is now closer to what Toronto was in its 1970s heyday: big enough to be metropolitan, variegated enough to be cosmopolitan, small enough to be knowable. Somehow it is significant, though unfortunate for the eye, that in 1997 Auckland's skyline came under the domination of the Sky Tower, an ugly needle-like structure similar to those in Toronto, Seattle, Calgary, and elsewhere. In the life of the contemporary city, it would appear, there comes a certain point when these structures, particularly if they contain revolving restaurants near the top, prove irresistible to the wowser class. In central Auckland, however, there is no need to look up. The city is human in scale, and what meets the eye at street level is often intriguing.

Travelling by freighter puts you in contact, first and primarily, with a city's waterfront. Such an area is often part of a larger industrial zone, often rundown and also quite a distance from the shopping, financial, and entertainment districts. Not so in Auckland, where ships tie up almost within sight of the intersection of Quay and Queen streets, the great commercial crossroads. The important shops often occupy the sort of pastel, colonial-style buildings from the turn of the century that are also common in Australia. These proceed in a straight line beginning at the Ferry Building, a baroque beauty, at the foot of Queen, at the water's edge. On the east-west axis, parallel to the docks, are elaborate fences with Neptune motifs and other traces of the old maritime culture. Such evidence, however, is mingled with signs of contemporary living. The traditional waterfront tattoo parlour, for instance, now does a bigger trade in faddish body art than in images of anchors and globes, and the strip joint is next door to a yoga centre of equal size. Some wonderful old shipping offices are found near by, such as the former headquarters of Northern Steamship, whose role in the development of New Zealand unfolds at the maritime museum across the street. This and another former shipping office are now occupied by advertising agencies. The waterfront has become trendy, one small indication of growing prosperity in the city and in fact the country as a whole, now that Britain has turned its commercial allegiance to the European Union and New Zealand has responded by becoming part of the Pacific Rim. "The first time I was here," one of the ship's officers told me, "you saw these creaky old British cars everywhere." Now, most of the cars, and many of the faces, and certainly much of the investment, are Japanese.

I would like to have visited the capital, Wellington, near the lower tip of the North Island, and then crossed the Cook Strait and gone on to Christchurch on the South Island, to see some of the wildly varying landscape in between. But I was tethered to the ship by the volatility of its schedule, which prevented me even from getting to the geysers and hot springs around Rotorua. Each day for three days, however, I was free to explore Auckland, with its ring of dormant volcanoes in the distance, and I came to the conclusion that New Zealanders have a pretty fine existence going for themselves. The verdict is not at all reluctant and is only confirmed by what I know of the societal organization.

Both the big islands have substantial Maori populations, of course, and New Zealand's present treatment of them, and its respect for their culture, have tended to set the standards for redress of wrongs done to aboriginal peoples. By comparison, the Aborigines of Australia and the First Nations of Canada have fared less well (though Canada may leap ahead when Nunavut, the Inuit homeland, finally comes into official existence in 1999). In all cases, the process is agonizingly slow. I happened to be in New Zealand during the run-up to a vote by 12,000 Ngai Tahu on the South Island on whether to accept a package that includes $100 million in compensation for past injustices, as well as 930 hectares of land (2,300 acres). The negotiations had been under way for six years. Mind you, the grievances extend back 150 years.

New Zealanders naturally wince and grind their teeth when frivolously compared to Australians. Auckland is as far away from Sydney as London is from Istanbul, New York is from New Orleans, and Toronto is from Winnipeg. Like Canadians and Americans, New Zealanders and Australians are horrified when the British cannot tell them apart (or so they pretend, we say to ourselves, suspiciously). Like Australia's, New Zealand's political climate is polarized. In both cases, the polarization is a result of the decision to join

Asia Pacific and embrace the future. Race and immigration are major issues. An anti-immigration political party is being formed in New Zealand, taking its inspiration from nativist bigots on the other side of the Tasman Sea.

New Zealand's role as a colonial power in its own right has become benign with time and practice, as seems only proper. Western Samoa (not to be confused with American Samoa, whose name tells its story) was once a German colony, until captured by the New Zealand military in the First World War. The Kiwis proved inept compared with the Germans; New Zealand's laxity, on one occasion, led to an epidemic of influenza that killed nearly one-quarter of the population. Western Samoa became independent in 1962, when Labour was in power in Wellington. The Cook Islands and a few other bits are virtually independent, but are governed "in association" with New Zealand, partly for reasons of economy. One is Tokelau. Another is Niue, one of the world's tiniest states, with a population of little more than 2,000 (down from 4,000 a quarter-century ago). At that, Niue is large compared with Pitcairn, a British colony, which is home to only a few score people, most of them descendants of *Bounty* mutineers. What's important is that New Zealand's stewardship of these places is not backed up by military threats, as with the French. I was actually surprised to see a naval vessel, the HMNZS *Something* (warships don't advertise their names), in Auckland harbour. (I was also surprised to run into Cadet Sarah from the *Pride of Great Yarmouth*, in mufti, sent ashore by the cook with a shopping list as long as a Chinese scroll. That could mean only one thing: fresh food for a while.)

New Zealand's politicians and media now speak of the lower Pacific as "the home region," a construct whose various parts differ wildly in their economics, from the sophistication of Australia to the example of Tonga, whose simple agricultural economy can barely sustain a growing population. Yet the hot-button issues are otherwise the same across this entire huge region: national identity, sovereignty, land ownership, aboriginal rights, and (especially in Fiji and Vanuatu) the role of women in policy-making.

Our departure from New Zealand was visually striking. We passed through the narrows, heading towards New Caledonia, almost due north, just above the Tropic of Capricorn. Night overtook us, and the Southern Cross was visible in the sky (exactly where it belongs).

∾

When Robert Louis Stevenson first laid eyes on Nouméa in New Caledonia in the 1890s, he remarked that it appeared to be built of old vermouth cases. Needless to say, a century of development has wrought great change, but probably less than a hundred years' worth would buy in most other places. Nouméa, at the southern end of Grande Terre, by far the largest of the New Caledonian group of islands, is a classic French colonial outpost, with a big markethouse and a smallish cathedral being the two magnetic poles of the local scene. Even with much recent building, enough of the old remains to show the perceptiveness of Stevenson's wisecrack. Short sections of central Nouméa, if viewed from flattering angles, look like the French Quarter of New Orleans after a rough night (which is all the more curious because the French Quarter is of course more Spanish than French, architecturally speaking).

For a variety of important reasons, New Caledonia is fundamentally different from Tahiti–Polynesia, which lies to the east. The local native residents are Melanesians, not Polynesians; in appearance, they're shorter, thinner, and darker skinned; in culture, customs, and language, more diverse. Just as obviously, Tahiti is where the French themselves (*les métros*) retire and make money from tourism, whereas New Caledonia is where they come to extract profit from mines, especially the giant open pits of La Société le nickel de Nouvelle-Calédonie, now a French state industry formerly owned by the Rothschilds. As we entered the harbour at Nouméa, after passing various atolls and islands on the way, we couldn't avoid seeing the bare terraces left by miners on the distant hills. The French refer to Grande Terre as *le Caillou* or *la Roche* – the Rock. The farther you move up the island, the more you see such scarring, as well as mine tailings, sulphur waste in streams, and general pollution in the air. The smelting operations turn out both ferronickel, used in making stainless steel, and matte, used in making high-grade steel for France's arms industry, because of its cobalt content. As it happens, all the matte is shipped to Le Havre, a regular port of call for the *Pride of Great Yarmouth* and its sister vessels. For reasons of colonial economics as well as strategic considerations, only French-flag ships are used in such cases, though small bits and pieces of general cargo are another matter. In fact, Nouméa is where the mystery of our dangerous freight was finally solved. After our first day in port, we were no longer flying Bravo from the mast, indicating that the explosives had been unloaded. Doubtless they were well on their way, if not to the nickel mines, then to the smaller iron-ore, cobalt, or magnesium mines on the west coast.

Another mystery was explained away when I struck up a conversation with the woman who ran the bureau de change at American Express. She was telling me about the small vicissitudes of living in an island society, any island society. "For example," she said, "we haven't had any onions in the market for weeks and weeks. Months. And you know how essential onions are to French cooking." Recalling the net sacks visible from my cabin window, I told her I had good news for her: the freighter on which I had arrived was carrying hundreds and probably thousands of kilos of onions. Judging by her reaction, I imagined her dashing down to the market as soon as the office closed at 1730.

By custom, ships at the overseas terminal at Nouméa leave their calling cards in spray paint on the wharf where they've been tied up. For example: "CS *Lavangna* Louie Henry B Nuri CE Martin B 5/4/96." CS stands for container ship, and the *Lavangna*, to judge by the graffiti, makes regular appearances. The names of the tradition-loving vandals who do the painting hints strongly at the mix of nationalities represented in a ship's crew: "CS *Singapore* Eng Guimbriena AB Cadauloo AB Seneres AB De Carbo 17/01/97." Another quaint tradition of the port is that the stevedores appeared to be as high as kites, especially those on the perhaps less-well-supervised night shift, when there is much loud tuneless singing, dropping of tools, and general barroom hilarity. Sometimes the crane operator nearest the superstructure would lose control for a moment and permit the huge hook swinging from his steel cable to crash against our first or second poop. The only real damage, however, seemed to be to the nerves of those on duty and the sleep patterns of those who were not.

At Nouméa we lost two more of the ship's company. An engineer named Anatoliy and our bosun, Gennadiy (I don't know the patronymics), had been hired for a new ship about to be launched at the former Lenin Shipyard at Gdansk, where Poland's Solidarity movement had its roots. They would fly Air Calédonie International to Australia and then back to Europe. Their good fortune had been known on the grapevine for some time, and though the engineer was not to be replaced, a new bosun had already been flown out by the company's staffing agency. Crew members told me that they thought Gennadiy was an excellent bosun "but he is from Georgia, and you know what the Georgians are like, always exaggerating the excellence of everything Georgian over everything Russian." They hoped for the best from his replacement.

The ever-unimaginative Captain Cook (one of whose anchors sits outside the now-closed marine museum in Nouméa) named the islands New Caledonia when he landed on the northeast coast of Grande Terre in 1774. The French, who followed in his wake, almost literally, then challenged the English to a game of political intrigue. Each side sent missionaries as the stalking horses of imperial ambition. The French, no doubt made anxious by Britain's successful colonization of New Zealand, won out eventually. They had a specific purpose in mind: to turn Grande Terre into a penal colony. Before the nineteenth century ended, about 20,000 convicts had been sentenced to an island in Nouméa Bay. In addition, nearly 4,000 political prisoners, mostly socialists and harmless philosophical anarchists, were interred on the nearby Île des pins (Isle of Pines) after the failure of the Paris Commune. By that time, the Société le nickel was already hard at work: the original inhabitants who lived near rich ore deposits were forced onto reservations, which police prevented them from leaving except to work the mines: a situation similar to that later associated with South Africa. The first rebellion broke out in 1878, setting off a long series of intermittent political crises that has marked New Caledonia's history right down to the present. Heavy taxation forced the free Kanaks, as they were called, into near servitude for the *colons*, who were planters and ranchers. The Melanesian population began a slow decline.

Progress towards independence has been slow, too. Not until after the Second World War did the New Caledonia Kanaks become French citizens, despite their valiant service in the First on France's behalf. Various other progressive moves followed, but they were nullified by de Gaulle. The result was an uprising in 1958, superseded by French political manoeuvres designed to keep the independence movement from gaining power. Violence flared in 1984 and again in 1989 and was put down by elite French troops. Matters have been relatively quiet for the past nine years, as the islands have been promised a vote on independence in 1998, as these words are being rewritten. While 45 per cent of the population is Melanesian and only 34 per cent European (with the remaining 21 per cent an exotic mixture of other races), this in no measure indicates how the voting will go, as the French who control the land and the capital also enjoy more electoral power. In any case, many observers feel that, whatever the outcome of the vote, the French, even the present socialist government, would never allow the New Caledonians independence. There is still too much money to be made here. Besides, the French (unlike the British, who have shied away from long costly colonial wars since Kenya) like to hold out until the last bullet has been fired and the last centime of profit repatriated. They've demonstrated that in Indo-China and Algeria.

With all this bubbling beneath the surface, I did not find Nouméa an easygoing port, for all the bougainvillea and hibiscus in bloom and all the signs of a quaintly mixed heritage, such as young women dressed in Mother Hubbards playing a three-hour game like rounders, which they insisted on calling cricket. We conducted our business, a matter of two and a half days, then headed northeast for Fiji, a place with quite a different history of recent political disturbance.

6

SUVA TO SANTO

*S*OMETIMES THE *Pride of Great Yarmouth* seemed to be coming to pieces beneath our feet. Little things kept breaking down. Doors came off their hinges, medicine cabinets fell crashing to bathroom floors. There was always more than enough hot water for showering, though. In fact, even the stuff from the cold water taps was hot. But one day the drinking water, which most definitely cannot simply be drawn from the boiler, went dry. Paradoxically, the ice-making machine was still up and running, so we were given extra buckets of ice cubes, which we put in the sun to melt. When it's twenty-eight degrees Celsius at nine in the morning, the process doesn't take long. Then, for a few days the lights began flickering. A rumour started to circulate that the primary bilge pump had ceased functioning temporarily. Despite this, we were luckier than the *Pride of Bournemouth*, which was following about six weeks behind us and, at last report, was laid up on the Pacific side of Panama with its diesel generators completely shot. No electricity, no refrigeration. There are captains who try to please the owners by keeping maintenance (that is, overtime) to a minimum. Then there are captains, like ours, who do otherwise. In the long run, one approach is probably no more economical than the other.

Normally, a youngish middle-aged cargo vessel of the *Pride of Great Yarmouth*'s size would benefit from UMS, or Unmanned Space, in the engine room, with conditions monitored at night only by computers. What we had instead were old-fashioned-looking alarm panels, with red lights that would blink and bells that would sound whenever a mechanical problem was identified. One of these boards was right above our heads in the dining room, next to the rather large portrait of the Queen. It provided only false alarms. One of its lights came alive every afternoon – as it had since the day we embarked from England – and the bells seemed to ring with perfect unpredictability day and night, stirring no one to action of any sort. I suspected an electrical short. In any case, as part of the *Pride of Great Yarmouth*'s Russian past, all the labelling on the system was inscribed in what Mrs. Murphy called "the acrylic alphabet." So it was, then, that we still used the ancient practice of manned four-hour watches. During daylight hours, all four engineers were on duty, and they spent the hours of darkness taking their turns in the engine room. Sometimes, when matters were not going well, a fifth person, the exalted chief engineer, pulled six-hour watches, while the chief mate hovered nearby like a head waiter.

At this point, en route to Fiji, matters were not going well. Some time during the middle of our forty-fifth night at sea, the engineer on watch heard a calamitous grinding sound in Number One engine, which abruptly stopped functioning. I confess that I slept through the excitement. The next morning a monoglot Russian, who was intimately acquainted with the problem, explained what happened to another Russian (bilingual), who translated the story into English for my benefit. "He is telling you that one of the big gears that kisses the camshaft" – I assumed that meant "meshes with" – "has two teeth broken off just like that." Another burst of serious-sounding Russian. "He says that, as you English say, trouble in engine room descends sky like cats and dogs." Our speed slowed to ten knots.

Ordinarily, cargo ships don't carry many spare parts. These only tie up operating capital and space. In our case, the exception was the extra propeller blades lashed down with chains to the main deck aft, and these came with the ship, like the spare tire on the back of a Land Rover. Otherwise, the policy is to make do, which for us wouldn't have worked. Fortunately, satellite communications were behaving tolerably at the time, and the captain was able to contact London, which was thirteen hours ahead of us. Did any of the sister vessels have an extra gear we could use? If not, could we simply borrow one from the *Bournemouth*, which was laid up at Panama City for what promised to be a while? Was the part (made in the Soviet Union, which no longer existed) stockpiled anywhere in Britain, or for that matter in the Russian Federation? If not, could London, having the specifications in the files there, find a firm of millwrights and founders to make an exact replica and then fly it to some port that is, as shipping people say, "on the fixture" (itinerary)? The gear, I learned, would weigh almost 800 kilos (1,765 pounds), including crate. That was probably too heavy for the type of small aircraft that serviced most of the ports in Papua New Guinea at which we called, except Madang, where air-cargo facilities were relatively sophisticated. Of course, there was always PNG's international airport, at Port Moresby, the capital, but Moresby wasn't really connected to the rest of the country by decent highway, only by small planes. Otherwise the best bet was Singapore, though all services were so expensive there that the company was known to avoid spending at that port if possible.

In the meantime, we neared Suva, the capital of Fiji, on one engine. Not that speed was a primary consideration. The approaches to the harbour are strewn with reefs, shoals, and protruding rocks, and caution is essential. I counted four wrecks in Suva harbour. One was a freighter with its deck awash and the bow and stern sections held together by only a thin ribbon of rusting steel; one day it will break in two. The next wreck had only its masts above the surface. The third was an old wooden vessel, an almost complete skeleton of ribs and beams, nothing else. It was hauled up on the shore not too far from our berth, where, in the very next slip, a longline trawler rested on the bottom, listing at a drunken angle.

I had never been to Suva. I had, however, previously visited Fiji's only other city, Nadi, at the opposite (western) end of the main island, Viti Levu. Nadi was then spelled Nandi. Somehow, during the mutiny and bloodless coup of 1987, the city lost one of its consonants, I'm not sure why. We tied up just before the light started to dim. Immigration formalities were informal in the extreme. Within a half hour I was ashore, where I bought a copy of Rupert Murdoch's *Fiji Times* and saw our arrival listed in agate type in the shipping-news column: *"Pride of Great Yarmouth*, from U.K. via Panama and Papeete, bound to Santo, Lae, Rabaul, Kimbe, Madang, and continental ports." This mention was in some sense a touching validation of our endeavours.

A memo from the captain was posted in the lounge and in the companionway outside the cabins. "Theft from accommodations is serious in all South Pacific ports," it read. "Suva is particularly bad. Here there is a recent history of both theft and assault on stewardesses aboard this vessel. In order to reduce the chance of theft, we will keep as many doors as possible locked from the inside, lock up bridge wing doors and bridge interior doors, lock up all valuables, leave only the starboard Deck No. 1 door open (near gangway)." The notice concluded: "The purser will ensure that the watch-keeping AB has a canister of fresh water and some cups. The deck ABs will keep them filled. Do not allow any dockers into the accommodations. Keep all cabins locked from the inside at night. Do not leave any cabin unattended without locking the door."

Duly warned, I proceeded into town as the crowded indoor day-market was giving way to the outdoor night-market, which was also thronged, and as the streets were beginning to fill up with – whom? There were East Indian pawnbrokers and Chinese ship chandlers, hucksters everywhere, Fijian men in their well-tailored wool skirts called *sulu*, street-corner evangelists and curbside moonshiners. The last of these sold old glass Coke bottles filled with what looked like urine and sealed with cork stoppers. They were lined up on the pavement outside the combined sailors' mission and bethel.

All of this activity took place against a backdrop of low colonial-style buildings. The handsomest is the 1930 clock-towered department store of Burns Philp Ltd., the most famous of the South Sea trading concerns, a company once as important in this region as the Hudson's Bay Company was in Canada or Jardine's in Hong Kong (and one whose shares are traded on the Suva go-go exchange as well as in Sydney). The structure is a perfect example of Pacific deco. Give or take a new office block or a multiplex cinema here and there, Joseph Conrad would respond to Central Suva on terms of comfortable recognition. "Malays and Lascars," I could hear him saying, inaccurately, in a Polish accent. "Malays and Lascars the lot of them."

Any elaboration of this thought was drowned out by the wonderful and crazy music pouring out of the honky-tonks. Like Tahiti, New Caledonia, Vanuatu, and other Pacific island cultures, Fiji has a robust local musical scene that combines traditional aboriginal sources with reggae, western influences, and modern mixing technology. The sound of each place is different and distinct, but is always found in the same two mediums – waterfront bars and locally manufactured audio cassettes. CDs, being more costly to make, are only for what Pacific islanders call international music, from Europe and America. These tapes seem like spontaneous outbursts of the people's limitless creativity, rather like the amazing mythological mural I saw in port that completely covered one of the steel containers about to be put aboard some ship. Process is always preferable to product. I'm much more attracted to such living sparks than to the "artefacts" and self-derivative, almost self-caricaturing carvings and crafts that fill the markets.

I also have my suspicions about the famous Fijian fire-walking ceremony to which tourists flock in such numbers, though at least this custom is interesting in that it's practised by Melanesians and Indians alike.

As I was to learn over the next few days, Suva at night is much different from Suva during business hours, when it reverts to being a prim place, and stately on a small scale, one so hot that people suffocate in their clothes. The difference between night and day there is a matter of tolerance as well as one of vibrancy.

I found the following observation in George Woodcock's *South Sea Journey* from a quarter-century ago: "Homosexuality is open and frequent in the islands where the culture is wholly or even partly Polynesian; I was accosted by male prostitutes in Apia, Nuku'alofa and Suva, but never in the true Melanesian islands or in Micronesia." Following this reasoning leads you to the fact that the native Fijians of Viti Levu and the more than three hundred smaller islands that make up the country are considered both Polynesian and Melanesian. The one strain complements or contradicts the other, depending on the question. Unlike the fully Polynesian people of Tahiti, they lack the tradition of *mahus*, or transvestites, who are an accepted part of street life in Papeete, and may or may not be gay (though one assumes that the crowds of them who hang about Papeete's dock gates are indeed). But neither are the Fijians puritanical to the extent of the Melanesians of Vanuatu, for example. Perhaps as a result, Fiji, and in particular Suva, have the South Pacific's only vibrant gay and lesbian community. Its existence also may have something to do with the British history of tolerance in sexual matters (Oscar

Wilde notwithstanding). Fiji became independent of Britain only in 1970 and still supports a large British expat community. It is perhaps the only place in the region where Europeans generally are permitted to immigrate, provided they invest the equivalent of US$50,000 (though even once accepted they are technically subject to arbitrary deportation). As Woodcock wrote in the 1970s (the date explains the masculine pronoun), any "white man who wishes to settle in Samoa and laze out his life there is no longer encouraged, any more than he is elsewhere in the South Seas. The beachcomber is almost extinct." This is even more the case today. Personally, I attribute some of Fiji's tolerance to the same factor that has bred its intolerance (and the political strife of recent years): the fact that it has become a multicultural society, to put the best face on the matter, or a polarized society, to speak more plainly.

In the last quarter of the nineteenth century, the scourge of the South Seas was blackbirding, the practice by white sea captains, who were little better than slave-traders, of contracting with (or kidnapping) Melanesians to work in the region's canefields. The American blackbirder Bully Hayes — Captain William Henry Hayes of Cleveland, Ohio, played in Hollywood film, most recently, by Tommy Lee Jones — was merely the most notorious of many. Black-birding was less a problem than evangelical Christianity or malaria, because it eventually faded away. Most of the unfortunate labourers were from the New Hebrides (another example of Captain Cook's genius for place-names), the present Vanuatu. Most of them were destined for Queensland, though 20 per cent of the total were sent either to New Caledonia or Fiji. The trade came to a halt with the introduction of the White Australia Policy of 1906, a course of sanctioned racism that remained in effect for half a century. Blackbirding was always of dubious legality. But it ran concurrently with a British policy of encouraging East Indian labour to migrate to Fiji for the same reason, to work the sugar plantations. The Indians stayed and prospered. Their descendants became the local merchant class, the stratum occupied by Chinese in other Pacific nations.

They also became, by the time of independence, a slight statistical majority of the population. With superior numbers came a desire for political power, which the Melanesians resisted. In 1987, however, a coalition of parties with Indians dominating formed a government, after winning nineteen of twenty-five seats in the legislature, more on the strength of their liberal platform than on the issue of race. One priority of the new government, for example, was declaring Fijian waters off-limits to ships carrying nuclear weapons. Following as it did similar bans by Vanuatu in 1982 and New Zealand in 1984, this initiative was a blow to the American government, which saw the Pacific gradually being closed to the U.S. Navy. There is a considerable body of circumstantial evidence of American support for the right-wing coup that came a month later, when Lieutenant Colonel Sitiveni Rabuka took control; later in the year, Rabuka struck a second time (without U.S. assistance) to consolidate his power before the governor general could call for an election. Rabuka suspended the courts, the press, and the unions, and tried to force Hindus and Muslims to convert to Christianity. The governor general stepped down and Fiji, at the insistence of India and others, was expelled from the Commonwealth. This in turn struck a profound blow to a nation so rooted in British culture that it remains to this day the only country where Prince Charles's birthday is a legal holiday.

The second coup seriously damaged the economy and caused an exodus of 50,000 Indians, one-sixteenth of the total population. Most went to Australia, New Zealand, or Canada. Civilian rule was restored in 1990 under a new constitution, recently reviewed and reconfirmed, that gives non-Melanesians equal status. The review process was just being completed at the time of our ship's visit. While the *Pride of Great Yarmouth* was in Panama, Fiji had been re-admitted to the Commonwealth. We would be in Vanuatu the following month when Prime Minister Rabuka, still in power but by due process this time, was scheduled to meet the Queen and apologize for the merry mix-up of ten years earlier. According to a report in the *Vanuatu Weekly*, he would present her with a whale's tooth as a token of contrition.

By now, we were beginning the part of the voyage that puts the tramp in tramp freighter. Up to and including Fiji, we were acting as a delivery service. There was a little back-loading to be done, especially in Suva, but basically we were supplying European manufactured goods to various SoPac ports. On this portion of the voyage, our corporate masters would go from customer to customer, contact to contact, soliciting island commodities for us to take back to Europe via Suez. This is the stage at which planning becomes impossible; reality becomes frustrating if you let it get to you, but assumes a carefree disposition if you are prepared to do the same, if you accept each revision of plans in a spirit of equanimity and adventure. In general, the *Pride of Great Yarmouth* managed to arrive on time; punctuality within a framework of unpredictability is essential to a tramp freighter, particularly to one seeking repeat customers. Our record was maintained despite the fact that we seldom, if ever, departed anywhere on schedule. Except for extremes of weather and mechanical contrariness, arrivals were within our control. Departures, by contrast, were scheduled at the discretion of the stevedoring classes. In Suva, we had time to kill, and I struck out for the botanical gardens and the Fiji museum.

Unfortunately, I caught the Thurston Gardens between blooming seasons, when the theatre is dark, so to speak, but this somehow only heightened the atmosphere of tranquillity. In the centre stands a gazebo with a clock tower bearing this inscription: "Erected by Henry Marks and Co Ltd in memory of their late director G. S. Marks, first mayor of Suva, who was drowned in the St Lawrence River, Canada, through the sinking of the SS *Empress of Ireland* 23rd May 1914." I assume that G.S. was of the family for whom Suva's Marks Street (along with Cummings Street, home to all the fascinating pawnshops) is named.

The Fiji Museum, opened in 1955, is the oldest in the South Pacific. It can hardly be called the most up-to-date or important without disparaging those at Papeete and no doubt other places. It takes the kind of old-fashioned approach to museology that seeks to wring importance out of individual treasures, treating the subject as an antiquary would, not as a historian does. What's wrong with this is that the story is well known and the exhibits are dusty and not always well cared for. Half of the space is dedicated to native Fijian culture, half to the period since European contact. Like most other island groups in this vastness of sea and coral – contemplating the Pacific Ocean makes you feel that God has too much free time – Fiji was found accidentally by a European who was seeking someplace else and didn't know where he was when he got there. In this instance, the European was Dutch: Abel Janszoon Tasman, who in 1643 was coming from New Zeeland, as it was spelled, on his way, he hoped, to the Solomon Islands. The reefs, the shoals, and the heavy surf precluded a landing at Fiji, and so off he went to Batavia. Tasmania and the Tasman Sea between Australia and New Zealand are named for him.

Among the artefacts in the museum are the wooden rudder and some metal bits from HMS *Bounty*, recovered in 1932 from the bottom of the harbour at Pitcairn, where the mutineers burned the ship in an attempt to avoid detection. Lead sheeting apparently covered parts of the *Bounty*, as a roll of the stuff, brought up at the same time, is also to be seen. The museum also possesses relics of Reverend Thomas Baker, a Methodist missionary killed and eaten by the Vatusila people of Fiji in 1867. This, perhaps the single most famous instance of cannibalism in the South Pacific, was probably a politically motivated murder. The Baker display case contains the sole of one of the reverend's shoes, which apparently proved inedible. (I think of Charlie Chaplin's famous repast in *The Gold Rush*.)

Meanwhile, back at the ship, there was uncertainty about where we would be going next and how long we would be there. This was simply the latest outbreak of doubt in an unpredictable business. Originally, when this voyage was being blocked out, there was a chance that we would be calling at Apia, the capital of Western Samoa (soon to be called plain Samoa), the fascinating one-time German colony so beloved of Robert Louis Stevenson. Not to dwell on the subject, but in Apia there is a shrine to Reverend John Williams, who began inculcating and fomenting Protestantism there in 1839 and was ritually devoured one year later in present-day Vanuatu (leaving his son to carry on). Apia was the first destination to fall off the fixture, however, for lack of what the shipping business calls "sufficient inducement." Next to go was Honiara on Guadalcanal in the Solomons, where Lever Brothers have enormous copra plantations (and also raise cattle – the two activities fit together nicely from an agricultural point of view). I had especially wanted to see Guadalcanal, because one of my uncles fought there with the U.S. Marines during the Second World War. Later, I believe, he came to administrative grief with the Corps. If I recollect the tale correctly from my childhood, he might well have been excommunicated from the Marines for excessive machismo. The next possible destination to fall away was Darwin, a part of Australia I've not seen, and the only part actually attacked by the Japanese in my uncle's time. Darwin remained a possibility up to the last minute, and we passengers had secured our Australian visas, as instructed. Historians today believe that Japanese expansionism in the Pacific was doomed to failure as soon as the United States entered the war; that Japanese strategic thinking was already shifting towards last-ditch defence of the home islands and away from empire building, with India as the ultimate prize. But that can't possibly be the way it looked in 1942. Brisbane, Sydney, and Melbourne so easily might have gone the route of Shanghai, Hong Kong, and Singapore, with the same awful toll in human life. Although personally a pacifist in my beliefs (devout, one might say), I think we have reason to remember what a remarkable thing our parents' and grandparents' (and uncles') generation did, fighting that war on both oceans at once, against two such fierce and determinedly wicked governments, both of which enjoyed nearly a ten-year head start in preparedness.

My fellow passengers and I had crammed, most of us, on the history and geography of Samoa and the Solomons, information it seemed we would never get to use. Then we were surprised to learn that the ship might be doing some unexpected business in Indonesia. The shock came in two waves. First there was a communiqué from the line's man in Lae, telling us that he had found a planter on Ternate Island who was willing to consign us two thousand tonnes of cocoa on pallets. No one on the ship had ever been to Ternate Island, if indeed anyone had ever heard of it. (The captain, in fact, had to order a new Admiralty chart to be delivered in PNG.) When I looked up the place in such reference books as could be found along the way, I was ashamed of my own ignorance.

Ternate and its less populous sister island, Tidore, only about a kilometre or half a mile apart, lie in the North Moluccas and were once Europe's only source of cloves. The clove trade, such as it must be, now centres on islands off Tanzania in East Africa. But Ternate was the hub when Sir Francis Drake visited there and came away much impressed by the sultan's harem. The Spanish, the Portuguese, and the Dutch fought for control in the sixteenth and seventeenth centuries. Before the Dutch finally triumphed, the Portuguese fortified the 10-kilometre (6.2-mile) circumference of Ternate. Most of this engineering was ruined in earthquakes, which are frequent there, or through the eruption of the 5,646-foot (1,721-metre) volcano named Gunung Gamalema, which has been losing its temper at intervals for the five hundred years for which records exist, and undoubtedly long before. The last time such a disaster threatened was in 1983. On that occasion, the son of the late sultan, Ish Kander Mohammed Jabir Shah, who died in 1975, rushed home, took the sultan's crown from the local museum, and carried it with him on a tour round the island. People credit the crown's magical properties with having kept rock, ash, fire, and lava from inundating them at that time.

A fascinating place, clearly, and so we were all dashed when our call there was cancelled. Then our hopes were raised, partway at least, by the possibility that we would take on cargo at another, rather better-known Indonesian port, Bandar Lampung, which is also interesting, though differently so. It is near Krakatau, the still-active volcano whose eruption in 1883 was felt as far away as Australia and whose effects reached even Europe, as clouds of ash circled the globe for the next three years. The largest explosion ever recorded at that time, the Krakatau disaster was also the first occasion on which people became aware of the potentially global consequences of such environmental catastrophes. Then suddenly Bandar Lampung also dropped off our list of destinations. The loss this time was owing to an entirely unexpected increase in copra exports and other products from drought-stricken Papua New Guinea, a place where conditions were becoming truly horrendous for the poor. The scattered jots of random intelligence that passed for news on the *Pride of Great Yarmouth* indicated that the Australian Defence Force had begun airlifting water, food, and medical supplies to large areas of PNG to avert a bigger disaster than the one already under way, which was tied to the El Niño weather cycle and the forest fires in Indonesia and elsewhere.

I was fascinated to see some of the telex traffic coming into the radio shack from the company's office in Lae. I saw only one side of the exchange, but I believe I got the sense of the whole by reading between the lines and ignoring the abbreviations I couldn't figure out.

To: Master, *Pride of Great Yarmouth*.
From: Lae.
Re: PNG etc.
Thanks your telex. All noted.
1) OK.
2) Noted. Will arrange for agents to land them to secure lock-up here.
3) Noted. Can you confirm if sufficient sep cloth on board to enable balance Madang copra to be loaded 2 TDS thus leaving 2 TDS clear for use elsewhere?
4) and 5) Noted. Will adjust rotation as shown in 6) below.
6) With the increase in copra ex PNG and requiring all 'tween decks bar 2P have now rearranged PNG schedule to include 2 calls Lae as follows: Alotau 06-07, Lae 09, Madang 11-12, Rabaul 14-15, Kimbe 16-18, Lae 19-20 with Singapore 30.
Kindly acknowledge. Regards. (This message may be incomplete.)

There was another flurry of questions and answers back and forth and then this telex.

To: Master, *Pride of Great Yarmouth*.
From: Lae.
Re: Your telex.
Thanks. All Noted.
1) Pls confirm arrangement to make it 0600 on 06 at Alotau.
2) At this time can advise that Tank No. 4 will not be required at Alotau. Most unlikely now that it will be required in Madang but Kimbe still remains a possibility for PKO if at all.
3) Will endeavour to obtain heating tape here otherwise arrange supply in Singapore.
4) Best way to handle radios is to land them at Lae c/o agents. What is physical size of them?
5) STS/DKE will attend for the copra bin at Lae.
6) Will advise agent about sludge but kindly back up with direct telex from Madang/Kimbe in due course.
7) The goal posts have moved again. Bookings from Kimbe now increased to 2470 T and Madang to 2100 T. We're now looking at the following. 1 TD Cocoa 650 T, 2 TDP empty at this time but possible 210 T copra to make up Madang figure, 2 TDS Santo copra 640 T, 2 LHP Santo copra 370 T, 2 LHS Santo copra 460 T, 3 TD PNG copra 2100 T, 3 LHP PNG copra 990 T, 3 LHS Santo copra 990 T, 4 LHP Santo copra 750 T, 4 LHS PNG copra 750 T, 5 TD cocoa 650 T. From above you will note that there is space in complete compartments for 4350 T copra which assuming shed clearance in Kimbe leaves space for only 1880 T ex Madang hence comments against 2 TDP.
8) Will you kindly check the drafts arr/dep Madang if we go to Madang after Kimbe? Max drafts at Madang is 10.1 metres [the *Pride of Great Yarmouth* fully laden draws 11.3 metres]. It may be rotation will have to be Rabaul/Madang/Kimbe/Lae in which case please advise.
Kindly acknowledge. Regards. (This message may be incomplete).

The way I interpreted these signals was that the great drought in PNG had somehow proved advantageous for the

Pride of Great Yarmouth, but that first we would be going to Santo – that is, the island of Espíritu Santo in the former New Hebrides, now called Vanuatu, a place whose principal exports, besides copra, are malaria, dengue fever, and hepatitis A. Tramp freighter indeed.

∞

There was a danger that the *Pride of Great Yarmouth* might arrive early in Espíritu Santo, largest of the 74 inhabited islands and cays (and 276 uninhabited ones) that make up the Republic of Vanuatu, 1,570 kilometres (975 miles) northwest of New Zealand. There was a danger, that is, of our arriving on a Sunday, when labour costs are prohibitive.

"It's a safe bet," said Sparks Murphy, drawing deeply on his Irish-American heritage, "that a place called Holy Ghost ain't normally open for business on the Sabbath." Sparks was correct, if for the wrong reason. The island was given its name by the Spanish navigator Luis Vaez de Torres in 1606, an astounding 168 years before James Cook entered these waters. Torres hoped he had found the elusive Australia, and so he christened the place Australia del Espíritu Santo in an act of wishful piety; today both the island and its town, Luganville, are usually called Santo for short. Torres's discovery notwithstanding, and despite the French presence here for many decades before independence in 1980, Vanuatu is overwhelmingly and devoutly Protestant evangelical in religion. But that doesn't dispute Sparks's main point, nor that of our captain, who decided simply to turn off our working engine and let us drift all day and all night until we could enter port first thing Monday morning.

At one point during the wait, Tim Beneke joined me on deck. The sea was so calm it seemed as though we were all in nothing bigger than a rowboat, rocking gently in some lake.

"In all my years in the U.S. Navy I never heard of such a thing – just sitting dead in the water like this, deliberately," Tim said.

"That might be one difference between the public and the private sectors," I said. Ships like the *Pride of Great Yarmouth* are acutely conscious of every tonne of fuel and every hour of berth time.

"I guess that's part of it," he replied. "Another thing is that our ships were steamers when I was in the service. You'd never shut down and let the boilers go cold. If you did, you'd need ten or twelve hours to get the steam plant up and running again."

Sparks, who dated from the same era, nodded in agreement.

Santo was the hottest place I had ever been to up to this point in my life, though I was told to expect the record to be broken in Papua New Guinea. Our purpose in going there was to take on four thousand tonnes of copra, the name given to the dried broken shells of the coconut, once the flesh and milk (the good parts) have been removed. Since the 1920s, copra has been one of the world's most lacklustre commodities, surpassed perhaps only by guano in both quantities and weak appeal. George Woodcock's *South Sea Journey*, which I had been carrying throughout my own South Sea journey, describes the plight of a copra grower in Western Samoa in the 1970s, when the stuff was already losing ground to "competition from temperate climate sources of vegetable oil such as mustard and sunflower."

Woodcock quotes one planter's lament: "I am getting only sixty-five talas a ton [at the time, about US$78]. . . . I have to pay eleven talas a ton for the copra to be cut and dried, and one tala a day for the workers who tend the plantation. Wages and the world market are killing the industry between them." Since then, "the industry" has gone downhill, but copra is still taken to mills in Europe, where the oil is squeezed out to make soap and cosmetics or to be sold as cooking oil. This shipping line has a contract to deliver the stuff to Le Havre. Related commodities are shredded coconut, which requires no explanation, and a substance called expeller, which is what's left of the poor coconut at the end of the copra process; it is pressed into pellets for use as animal food, mainly in Europe.

Ships operating under collective agreements with the Seafarers' International Union in the United States actually must pay bonuses to crews handling copra, just as they do in the case of those handling explosives or toxic chemicals or radioactive materials. The stuff smells terrible. At first whiff, one is reminded of suntan lotion, for that is one of the products in whose manufacture copra is used. After a while, though, the scent is more like that of rancid butter; it would overpower the ship, its crew, and passengers for the remainder of the voyage. Expeller, which is shot into the holds through powerful hoses, has the added disadvantage of being extremely dusty as well – so dusty that the dockers and crew should really be wearing masks to protect themselves. But the main hazard of coconut products is fire. If they have not been truly and thoroughly dried before being stowed, they tend to smoulder in the holds and combust spontaneously. Thermo-couples are inserted into the cargo, and they are supposed to signal a big rise in temperature. In addition, crew members sometimes measure the temperature in the holds by hand. Such methods seem to perform better in theory than in practice.

The agent who came aboard at the port of Santo/ Luganville brought us mail and also a week-old copy of the *International Herald Tribune*, in which I learned of the death of James Michener, aged ninety. Michener made and gave away fortunes from his books, especially from the rights to *Tales of the South Pacific*, which became the musical *South Pacific* and was based on his experiences while stationed in Santo during the Second World War. Reading his dreadful prose is like trying to eat dry corn flakes, but he was a kindly, humane, and insatiably curious person, and I tried to picture him in Santo in 1942. The place was hopping then, with as many as a hundred thousand U.S. servicemen at any one time. (Another of them, before he was transferred to the Solomon Islands, was a young Navy lieutenant, John F. Kennedy. I can't help but suppose that the shock of coming to Santo more or less straight from Harvard may help explain the satyriasis and other moral complaints from which he suffered in later times.) I made a little pilgrimage to the huge old banyan tree under which the original of Michener's principal character, Bloody Mary (so called because her teeth were red from chewing *buai*, or betel nut), used to preside. I guess I needn't have gone so far, for in some sense it is always 1942 in Santo, and always will be.

Loading four thousand tonnes of copra is a lengthy business, especially considering the system in place at Santo. Whereas at some other ports we would be taking on

consignments from large-scale planters, here we were
dealing with small freeholders, members of a local co-op,
who arrived in beat-up Japanese four-by-fours with as few
as ten or twelve large burlap sacks of the awful stuff and a
few friends or family members to help them. At the co-op,
each truck is weighed on arrival and departure, with the
difference in weight credited to the farmer's account. The
bags are emptied into big steel hoppers, which are then
moved to the dockside by fork-lifts. Local stevedores, using
the shipboard cranes, swing the hoppers one at a time into
first one hold and then another. Down in each hold is a crew
of five ni-Vanuatu, who unhook the chains on two of the
corners so that the contents can be tipped out. A bit always
remains in the hopper, which the crane operator then
swings crashing into the bulkhead. In the end, the crew have
to climb inside the hopper and unload the rest manually.
Each five-man crew has only one shovel, so most must use
their hands and feet as tools.

"This looks like some sort of job-creation program,"
said Sparks in disgust.

After every two metres or so of copra has been put in a
hold, the crane operator picks up one of the two little bull-
dozers owned by the co-op, so that the copra can be
smoothed out. For reasons of economics as well as fire
safety, it is essential that the cargo be well tamped down,
eliminating air pockets and maintaining a perfectly flat top
surface. During the course of the first day, however, both
cats broke down. One developed engine trouble; the other
threw one of its treads, which lay spread out in the hot sun
like a skin shed by a snake. At this point, to keep things
moving, the ship's own crew and all the local stevedores had

to climb down into the holds, using their hands and feet and whatever garden tools could be found to push the foul-smelling stuff back under the lips of the hatches and into all the cracks and hollow spaces, creating a hard, flat surface for the next layer to rest on. "Here we are at the start of the new century almost, and look at us," one of the people lamented. "We're down on our hands and knees, moving the rotting stuff around like we were Stone Age people." Then it began to rain. The holds had to be covered and the waiting hoppers driven under cover in the warehouse. In a while the showers let up and the hatches were opened to the sky again. The fork-lifts emerged from hiding. Half an hour later the rain resumed. The game of hide-and-seek continued the rest of the day, well into the night, and part of the following morning. I found it prudent to explore the island.

Luganville's hard currency comes mostly from scuba diving. In the Second World War the U.S. government expropriated the 22,000-tonne, 210-metre-long (690-foot) luxury liner the *President Coolidge* for use as a troopship. On October 25, 1942, it struck an American mine at Santo and began to sink. It sank so slowly that all 5,150 Marines on board made it to safety, but it took down with it several of the ship's company. It is now the world's largest divable wreck, and attracts enthusiasts from round the world. The prow is 21 metres (69 feet) underwater, with the hull sloping downwards from there. Too deep for me. But Tim, an expert diver, took an excursion to the site and returned full of excitement. "The holds are stacked with M-1s, helmets, canteens, everything, just as they left it. One of the most amazing things I've ever experienced."

Before independence, Vanuatu was a British and a French colony simultaneously. As a result, the ni-Vanuatu speak English and French as well as Bislama, the local pidgin; one of Vanuatu's two weekly newspapers is published trilingually. This odd power-sharing, formally established in 1906, was called the Condominium, but popularly known as either the Conundrum or the Pandemonium government. In *South Sea Journey*, George Woodcock explains how what he calls "the flavour of comedy" began on his arrival at the airport, "where we were faced not with one but with two immigration desks. One was for French subjects and was administered by a trio of kepi-crowned gendarmes; the other, at which we were processed, was for Commonwealth subjects, and a New Hebridean sergeant in khaki with a bastard glengarry bonnet on his head stamped our passports under the supervision of a dyspeptically melancholy British officer." Elsewhere, Woodcock saw "a flagstaff with double halyards and pullies, so that both flags may fly, and when there is a ceremony at which both Commissioners appear, they ascend the steps together with measured steps and, as in some stately ballet, turn so that they face the audience simultaneously." He went on:

> the British and French administrations are equal but separate. They maintain their own police forces and courts. British residents can only be arrested by their own police and tried in their own courts, and the same applies to the French, but foreigners – which usually means Americans – and native New Hebrideans are fair game for either. A limited number of matters of common concern, such as the customs and postal services and transport, are handled by the Condominium, and the Condominium is also responsible for the Joint Court which assesses land-claims by

both foreigners and natives; in typical New Hebridean style, the impartiality of the Joint Court was guaranteed originally by the appointment to the Presidency of a deaf Spaniard who spoke neither French nor English. . . .

When U.S. troops departed in 1945, they tried to sell to the Condominium all the trucks, earth-moving equipment, pontoon bridges, and the like that they had brought in so laboriously. But dealing with the Condominium proved frustrating. When the final offer – eight cents on the dollar surplus price – was refused, the Americans took all this stuff that would have been so useful eventually to the slowly emerging ni-Vanuatu and dumped it in the ocean from barges. Hence the local attraction named Million-Dollar Point (or, sometimes, Billion-Dollar Point), where the debris begins right on the beach and continues out for hundreds of metres. The wall of rusting steel has become an artificial reef that is home to dozens of varieties of tropical fish and other marine life. The snorkelling – more my style – was excellent. I saw large crabs nesting in old Jeep crankcases.

Visiting divers completely fill up Luganville's one decent hotel and two western-style cafés, and keep in business two dive shops and thirty taxi drivers (sharing about ten cabs). If one must have tourism, this is the sort to have, as the divers keep to themselves and do not disrupt the local culture or environment. Otherwise, Luganville is a place that has remained still, chronologically speaking – if indeed it has not actually slipped backwards since independence, given the bouts of political discord since then. Vacant buildings are numerous along the long dusty main street connecting the wharf to the markethouse. But the ones still in business tickled me with both their sameness and their sweet diversity.

Most of the stores are Chinese. "Lo Chi Lin, General
Merchant and Island Trader" says one signboard. Most are
supplied by other island traders from small coastal vessels
whose owner-operators get their wares from the giant
trading firms such as Burns Philp, Morris Hedstrom, and
Steamships Pty. As a result, there is a familiarity about their
core inventory. But what an inventory. The typical estab-
lishment sells groceries, fireworks, bolts of cloth, fishhooks,
anvils, western and Chinese patent medicines, pictures of
the Virgin Mary suitable for framing, a dazzling variety
of bolo knives and machetes, bicycle chains, parts for obsolete Primus stoves, gents' and ladies' underwear, stationery,
audio cassettes, and 5-kilo (11-pound) tins of ships' biscuits,
known locally as cabin biscuits. The newspapers publish
an annual cyclone-season advertising supplement, in which
such merchants stress the superiority of their kerosene
lamps, lamp wicks by the metre, torches, and candles. Following the old French colonial practice, the other businesses in Luganville close for a three-hour siesta during the
hottest part of the day, 1130 to 1430 hours. Chinese shopkeepers, however, remain open; they merely turn off the
lights and do business in the dark.

There is only a handful of European residents. Typical
is the Australian foreign-exchange dealer and gambling-
club operator. Another is the island bootlegger. Westerners
who wash ashore in Luganville tend to love it or loathe it.
Personally, I loved it. I found myself winding down to
match its pace, which is slow-motion. And since even slow-
motion activity here is sudorific, you are best to stay out of
the sun and avoid unnecessary exertion. Sundown brings
some relief, but also signals the pestilential mosquitoes.

CAUSING SWEAT

Whether they like or dislike the place, Europeans usually remark on the unaffected and genuine friendliness of most ni-Vanuatu. We were so long in getting all the copra aboard that I began to make some acquaintances in town. One of them took me into his confidence enough to let me tag along with him to a kava bar, a place where whites are not normally found.

Kava is a drink that looks like yesterday's bilge and tastes worse than dishwater. It is not alcohol but rather a non-addictive herbal drug, made from the dried root of the pepper plant (*Macropiper methysticum*). In Fiji, Tonga, and Western Samoa, as in Vanuatu, it is drunk from coconut shells as part of elaborate rituals, which are sometimes watered down (like the kava itself) when tourists come by. The ni-Vanuatu consider the stuff consumed in Fiji, Tonga, and Western Samoa to be fit only for weaklings. In Santo, where kava is a matter of daily routine as well as an integral part of certain special occasions, the stuff is potent indeed. The best of the best is still made the old-fashioned way, by perpetually stoned children who extract the juice by chewing the root, mixing it with their saliva.

A visitor wouldn't even know that kava bars exist until well after dark, when they somehow silently make themselves known to interested parties, like booze-cans in Toronto. The one my friend took me to was on a dirt road well outside town and seemed nothing more than the site of a mellow gathering. Inside, the two-room house was in darkness. People were smiling, nursing their shells. My buddy entered first and somehow prepared the way for my appearance. He even bought the first round, which numbed my mouth like Novocain. The second and third rounds

(my shout, as the Aussies say) carried the feeling, or rather
lack of feeling, to my legs and feet. Normally there is no kava
takeaway, but after my companion put me in the passenger
seat of his beat-up ute he went back inside and returned with
a gift – a 1.5-litre water bottle filled with the stuff. My grat-
itude amused him as much as my slowed speech and movement trying to express it. He dropped me off at the dock
gate, where a security guard understood the situation in-
stinctively and helped me get started up the gangplank.
I counted fifty-six steps. It was raining again.

Many of the buildings in Luganville began life as Quonset
huts. Out in the countryside, as you head north up the
valley of the Saranata River, numerous earth-sheltered
Quonsets, which the U.S. military once used as ammo
dumps, have now become barns for Brahma cattle. Such
animals are required to keep plant-growth from choking the
coconut palms; they have also become a second source of
income – beef for export to Japan. Scattered here and there
throughout Santo are the wrecks of aircraft, both fighters
and bombers, on which the faint markings "U.S." or the
symbol of the Rising Sun are still visible. There are also
many airstrips built by the Americans, all of them now
deserted, some with large trees growing in the middle of the
runways. I wouldn't compare them to the Roman roads of
Britain, but after more than a half century, most of these
landing places, whether of blacktop or concrete, are still
holding together well, so soundly were they engineered.
That's what you notice about them first. What strikes you
next is how short they are by modern standards.

Vanuatu has known war of sorts since the Big One. When
the country was still called the New Hebrides and ruled

jointly by the British and the French, the former were willing, even eager, to grant independence. But the latter were too reluctant. Throughout the 1970s, the level and complexity of political intrigue and conspiracy on these islands must have resembled that of a papal court in medieval times, as various factions plotted for control, making unlikely allies and enemies. The central figure in many ways was Jimmy Stevens, who had both Tongan and Scots blood and was headquartered at Fanafu, a tiny village near the centre of the island, on the fringe of a peanut-growing area. It was a village I was eager to see, as this was where the so-called Coconut War started, the event that led to independence in 1980, but only after a series of startling developments, such as the burning and sacking of Luganville. At one point, British and French troops were replaced by a force from Papua New Guinea, which shelled the Santo shoreline. Their arrival marked the first time in the twentieth century that one South Pacific nation had invaded another. The Papuans arrested Stevens and seventy others. Stevens was sentenced to fourteen and a half years in prison and died in 1994. He continues to be a subject of controversy, in part perhaps because he seemed to side with both political extremes in turn. He was seen first as a socialist threat, and many of the leftist reforms he called for were implemented by the new government of a free Vanuatu. Later he allowed himself to be armed and equipped by U.S. rightists who were looking for a puppet state in which to test their theories of a taxless society. Because he was charismatic and accepted military goods from white foreigners, Stevens was described by his enemies as the leader of a cargo cult. He wasn't. But in the South Pacific this is a term charged with enormous emotion.

Cargo cults are a favourite research project of American cultural anthropologists, who usually manage to dismiss or play down their purely political significance. The core idea behind the South Pacific cargo cults is that "natives" discover or are given "cargo" (western manufactured goods) and, extrapolating from this, develop a belief that a sort of messiah will reappear from overseas and shower them with the trappings of materialism. No one is certain how far back these recurring folk beliefs extend, but in this form, probably not before the arrival of Christian missionaries in the early nineteenth century. The island of Tanna, one of Vanuatu's most popular destinations, is home to the Jon Frum cult, which came alive again during the Second World War on Efate, the capital island. Local Melanesians employed by the U.S. armed services saw African-American GIs being issued the same materiel as whites, an experience that led somehow to a revival of old (pre-missionary) traditions and beliefs. These found expression in the idea that one Jon Frum (that is, John *from* America) would appear to distribute western goods among the poor. Such cults had clear anti-colonial subtexts, and the British imprisoned the cult leaders at Port Vila on Efate – in the long run, to little avail. After Prince Philip visited the New Hebrides in the 1970s, one group on Tanna, about three hundred strong at present, came to see HRH as the reincarnation of Jon Frum. There is even an altar to him.

Cargo cults are not confined to Vanuatu. New Hanover in Papua New Guinea is renowned as home to a cargo cult that worships Lyndon Johnson, of all people. Not Hubert Humphrey or Walter Mondale, *Lyndon Johnson*. What's most remarkable, though, is the way the cultural tide ebbs and flows. Some anthropologists are cargo cultists in reverse;

they see themselves enriching us all by getting in touch with "primitive peoples." Pentecost in PNG, for example, is famous as the island where bungee jumping (using vines tied to the jumper's ankle) originated as an ancient rite. Just as it took the Melanesians to find religious significance in old Coke bottles and the other detritus of western culture, so it took the Euro-Americans to transform the sacred into a mere sport through the application of modern bungee technology and marketing.

Fanafu is where Jimmy Stevens was captured. This makes the spot special, though in appearance it remains the typical Vanuatu village, with thatched huts (which need to be rebuilt every five or six years) forming a circular area in which both hens and naked children run and play. When I visited, an elder, wearing only some leaves around his waist, offered me a greeting and asked for a contribution towards the cost of digging a new well, which I could see was under way, in soil that turned to clay a metre or so down, although the earth seemed so rich and black on the surface. The women kept out of sight during my visit, except to peek around doorways at the tall, pale stranger.

Slash-and-burn agriculture is still practised on Santo, and the air is bitter with smoke from strategic fires. Logging has become an important business, and the roads are deeply pitted from the heavy trucks running back and forth to the sawmill at Luganville. Yet the natural order is always re-asserting itself. Hibiscus and bougainvillea are in blossom everywhere. Fence posts, stuck in the ground, in time take root and come alive again.

Hidden back in the bush are some odd survivors from an earlier stage of civilization. The most memorable was a tough old Australian, who gave the impression that he had simply stayed on after the Second World War. With his young ni-Vanuatu wife (probably his third or so, judging by the difference in their ages), he operated a hilariously anti- quated little steam-powered mill for extracting oil from coconuts. The set-up was a rusty cast-iron affair with many flywheels and belts. He had to run all the kernels through the machine three times before the job was done. His rela- tionship with this bizarre piece of nineteenth-century tech- nology reminded me of Humphrey Bogart and his steam launch in *The African Queen*.

Descending back into Luganville, I passed two equally depressing institutions. One was the prison, an almost windowless rectangle built facing the exercise yard inside. The other was the hospital, which seemed dirty and poorly furnished. Patients sat on lawn chairs outside the TB ward, looking weak and forlorn. The day before my journey, one of the ship's engineers suffered a shoulder injury on duty and had to be brought to the place for an X-ray to determine whether he had sustained a fracture. The answer, fortunately, was negative; but he reported back saying that an X-ray was just barely within the technological reach of the hospital.

A surprise awaited me back at the *Pride of Great Yarmouth*. In the four days we had been at Santo, laboriously taking on a thousand tonnes of copra each day and evening, we had picked up some more business elsewhere. Instead of going straight to Papua New Guinea, the focus of our voyage, we would first go to Efate to pick up cargo at Port Vila.

I was sorry to be leaving Luganville. From a first im- pression of disappointment, I had come to be fond of the place, with its half-deserted Wild West atmosphere, its generous and friendly citizenry, its air of dilapidation, and its tiny, tiny branch (the world's smallest?) of the Alliance Française. May it always remain what I saw. A big hotel and a decent airport would ruin it – will do so soon, no doubt.

Port Vila was a twelve- to fourteen-hour run on our one working engine. We departed at 1600 hours and were there when I awoke in the morning. The port itself is a harbour within a harbour, with the main island, which is much greener and hotter than Santo, ringed by numerous smaller ones. The town is big and prosperous enough to seem stressful after Luganville. The French influence is much stronger here, in language, architecture, and investment (though the Aussies, I noted once more, control the lucrative foreign-exchange market). There is the usual wreck in the harbour: this time, a capsized hull like a dead whale; I suppose that, once the insurance claim was paid, no one bothered to remove it. I found an Aussie pub at the far end of town and watched the news on CNN. It sounded like the same news that was on when I departed Canada months ago. The main street is narrow and zigzags along the contours of the harbour. Its sharp angles contribute to the feeling of congestion, a sensation that seemed almost surreal after Luganville, where traffic stops when a dog pauses in the street to scratch at a flea. How quickly did the tension of western culture recede under Santo's unrelenting sun. How quickly did it reappear at the slightest reminder of the world I was running away from.

7

PAPUA NEW GUINEA:

RATS AND BUTTERFLIES

*A*FTER SIXTY-TWO DAYS on the ship together, we passengers were still discovering new facts about ourselves, about one another, and about freighter travel. For example, people at sea become fascinated by the weather, because it has such a direct bearing on their quality of life. High-pressure systems, squall lines, odd cloud formations like stalactites and stalagmites – for us, these were matters of intense discussion and concern in a way that they would not have been on land. At some stage, I imagine, all ten of us (reduced from eleven by Molly's departure) had begun making mental lists of the comparative advantages and disadvantages of sea travel. A big advantage, I'm sure we would all agree now, is that it limits your contact with bureaucracy in whatever country you visit (whereas air travel only increases the red tape). When we neared a port, the purser would collect our passports; then *he* would fill out all the forms and make declarations on our behalf – sometimes over a drink with the customs and immigration people, in his office. Because ours was not primarily a passenger ship, we civilians were human cargo, in transit, just passing through; even though we might spend three or four days ashore with complete freedom of movement, we were never, strictly speaking, "landed." In such circumstances, most countries don't bother to stamp your passport. Even the notoriously officious New Zealand authorities hardly noticed.

If freighter travel cuts down on this kind of bother, it also fosters another variety of nuisance: the social kind. My experience has been that the more expensive or crowded the form of public transport – bus, train, commercial aircraft – the more it is permissible to give others one's life story. (On a plane, especially in business class, one could say to one's neighbour, "My, that's an interesting facial scar. Where did you acquire it?" On a bus, such a lapse in etiquette can be lethal.) Freighter passengers tend to blur these distinctions, because most of them are trying to convince themselves they are actually aboard cruise ships or luxury liners. Such middle-class fantasies on a working vessel gave me the fantods, as Mark Twain used to say. Yet the shipping line goes along with the delusion, encouraging unnecessary conversation among incompatible people. On our first boarding, the purser gave everyone a list of all the other passengers and urged us to chat up one another. I found this both painful to experience and sad to witness. They even put your name on your cabin door, as though you were a public convenience. We were expected to, well, mingle. Interact. I found the image, like the prospect, terrifying.

Personally, if I had had my way, we would have all been anonymous, like participants in a masked ball, or people on a bus going to El Paso. Of course, we'd come together for meals and boat drills – but in the blessed silence of a Trappist monastery. Instead, everyone confessed, to everyone else, his or her life story, goals, medical history, expectations, reasons for being aboard, likes, dislikes, turn-ons, and turn-offs. The passengers chattered constantly, like just-rescued castaways from an international Gilligan's Island. The only time they really stopped nattering was when their turn at cards or some board-game required their utmost concentration. Generally speaking, the group was not composed of self-sufficient personalities with serious thinking to engage in. Clearly, given, for instance, my banishment to the officers' table, I had not endeared myself to at least one of them, and for their part, they, with one or two or maybe three exceptions, had been driving me batty for sixty-two days – and we were still only halfway to wherever we were going. Yet I cannot deny that adversity had caused us to – how cautiously I employ the word – bond.

Curiously, the process began with the American woman in her late fifties, the one whom I had privately called Seagrams since our second day out, when, passing her cabin, I noticed that she was doing her best to boost the export of Canadian Club. She also played Scrabble a great deal, and frequently lost her temper, because she could never beat the British passengers. They knew so many more words and, what's more, had a generalized grasp of English spelling. Her main activity, however, was the bottle. She seemed to buy in bulk from the slop chest (I could hear her orders being delivered) and from local merchants whenever we were ashore. When she ran out, she would cadge (a good Scrabble word, *cadge*) drinks from the others. Vodka, gin, sherry if necessary, even Kiwi wine in three-litre boxes.

This was nobody's business, including mine, so long as she confined her excesses to her cabin. But then she began turning up roaring drunk at breakfast, lunch, and dinner, holding on to the chairs and tables to navigate the room (even when we were tied up securely in some port). Again, this was none of our affair, except perhaps to express concern for her safety, as a moving ship is dangerous enough for those who are sober. At this point in the voyage, though, as we sailed for Papua New Guinea, she was on a real bender, replete with disturbing absences and equally disturbing appearances, during which she would get the *Pride of Great Yarmouth* into an uproar. She'd burst into spontaneous tears or make a clumsy pass at a crew member and then not remember doing so; or she would start bizarre arguments that would prompt even the most patient person to walk out. "On farms in Europe, you know, they don't have barns like we do in America!" Whenever she expressed this particular thought – apropos, I might say, of absolutely nothing – we all knew what was coming.

The time before last, Mrs. Murphy leaned over the table and whispered in my ear. "I've been expecting something like this," she said. "I've been waiting for the other sock to drop!"

When Seagrams next began to rant about agricultural outbuildings, I was the only person in the dining room, having dragged myself down there early, precisely so I could avoid her at breakfast. She came in, taking a zigzag course, and collapsed in the chair next to me. She shouted back to the galley for food, then began crying. She startled and embarrassed me by asking me to take her hand, which I awkwardly did. She had obviously been weeping on and off for much of the night. She had panda eyes, two black rings, diverting attention from her drinker's nose, which looked like the kind of folding road map that shows all the secondary highways in red. She told me how she had been in rehab several times and thought she had the problem licked. But since being on the ship, she had been experiencing recurrences of an old liver condition, her first in eight years. She knew the medical problems were back full force. As she no longer had a current prescription for the highly specialized drug she had been taking, she had been self-medicating with booze. Still sobbing, she staggered out of the room just before the arrival of her food, which I had to send back, struggling with Russian-English pidgin.

I knew she hadn't confided in me out of affection, for I was her least favourite shipmate and the target, ultimately, of many of her farming monologues. Although I felt that I had to treat what she told me confidentially, I concluded that it would be best if I had a word with the purser. While I was not expecting him to be surprised by any news of the bender, he was no doubt unaware of the resurfacing of the old medical condition and might have some practical suggestions.

Maybe the necessary drug, sophisticated though it sounded, was available in Port Moresby in Papua New Guinea.

"You haven't been to Moresby, then, I take it?" he asked sympathetically.

"Singapore? Surely Singapore."

"That's a very long way in the future."

"I know, but maybe you should consider making arrangements for her to get ashore and see a physician?"

The purser looked dubious and reminded me that, on boarding, everyone had presented a certificate of good health and also absolved the shipping line of any liability for accidents or sickness during the voyage.

To make a long story palatable, the purser finally agreed to stop selling Seagrams any more spirits from the ship's store. Later, he prevailed on another passenger, the retired doctor, to give her Dramamine every night. This drug for motion sickness would also help her sleep. When the patient didn't turn up for meals two days in a row and didn't respond to raps on her door, the purser, with one of the stewardesses carefully in tow, very reluctantly opened her cabin with the master key to find her sleeping and apparently all right. Mrs. Murphy spoke for us all when she said, "I'm glad she's okay. I was afraid she might have OJ'd in there."

For the next several weeks Seagrams remained pretty sober, though this did nothing to improve her personality. Her closest apparent friend on the *Pride of Great Yarmouth* was the New Age woman from Denver. Even she eventually lost control of her cheerfulness and said to Seagrams, "You know something? You're a real bitch when you're drinking, but you're a bitch when you're sober, too."

New Age repeated the comment when telling me the story, explaining how difficult she found the words, despite feeling she had to say them in an attempt to keep her shipmate from following an even more self-destructive path. Suddenly I had a new respect for New Age. She might be a little lacking in polish, I said to myself, but she has a good heart. I began to view the others with equanimity as well.

Sparks, Tim, and the doctor have recurred often enough in this narrative to produce mental pictures in the reader's

mind, I hope. Mrs. Murphy as well. As I run down the list
of them in my head, I see that the passengers, except for
myself, were all in the computer or health-care fields (or,
like Mrs. Murphy or the doctor's wife, were married to
people who were). Seagrams and New Age both worked for
health-management organizations in the United States,
for example. Seagrams will be one of the stock characters
of late-nineties fiction when it comes to be written – the
downsized worker who "took the buy-out at fifty-five."
New Age, considerably younger, had been married several
times. Once to an Italian, once to an Iranian, a third time
to someone whose nationality I didn't catch. One or more
of them left her a widow, with money to travel some
months every year on exotic rail or sea trips.

The real delights were Jane from Yorkshire and Roberta
from Scotland, both sixty-two or so, and both former
nurses. They had known each other since they were young
girls during the war. Jane was the victim of a motor accident that had left her paralysed in one leg, and also, I gather,
gave her money to travel, sometimes with Roberta as her
companion, sometimes with another friend, and sometimes
on her own. Jane and Roberta were both experienced
freighter travellers. Jane had gone down the whole coast of
West Africa on a German vessel, for example; Roberta was
virtually the only passenger on a fully containerized P&O
ship from Britain to Hong Kong. "On fully containerized
ships," she said, "the captain is really reduced to little more
than an administrator." The two women spoke knowledge-
ably about various shipping companies and ports. They
could speak to the differences found among the NYK Line,
Mitsui, Germanischer Lloyd, and European Marine. Real

pros at running away to sea. They were also delightful in and of themselves, full of kindness, charity, patience, good sense, and, occasionally, some wonderful Old Country turns of phrase. Looking up at the cloudy sky one day, Jane said, "There's not enough blue there to patch a Dutchman's trousers, is there?"

One of the reasons that some of us might have been a trifle on edge – and another reason why it's reassuring to have a good supply of former health-care people on hand – is that all of us had been taking anti-malarial chemo-prophylactic drugs. We needed them in our systems for Vanuatu, the beginning of the dreaded Melanesian malaria belt, and all of us, in one way or another, had been ill from one or more of the various side-effects, which ranged from the intestinal to the psychological.

Malaria has been an evil in this part of the world for centuries, and the bleak situation has steadily worsened in recent times. Each year, between 300 million and 500 million people worldwide are infected by the mosquito-borne disease; between 1.5 million and 2.7 million of them die from it. It is a poor person's disease, not lucrative to treat. It is probably most common in Africa, where development is less rapid, but much of Asia and the Pacific are seriously affected as well. The zone that begins at Vanuatu takes in all of Papua New Guinea, Indonesia, the Malaysian Peninsula, the Indian Ocean, and the Mid-East along the Red Sea and the Suez Canal – in short, our entire itinerary until we would finally arrive in the cooler Mediterranean. Malaria's resistance to older drugs is growing quickly, and in some countries more quickly than others. There are various reasons. Brazil, for example, hastened the uselessness of

chloroquine, once the standard means of malaria pre-
vention, by adding it to the country's supply of table salt.

In British colonial times, taking quinine was the prudent
course. The English mixed it with gin to kill the taste, thus
accidentally inventing the gin-and-tonic. In the Second
World War, troops in such theatres of operations as Burma
were issued a drug called Mepacrine, which worked
reasonably well but had unfortunate side-effects. It turned
your skin as yellow as aged bamboo, caused impotence, and
with prolonged use could lead to loss of teeth and hair.
Later in the war, research produced chloroquine phos-
phate. A weekly 300-milligram dose was the standard
preventive measure until comparatively recently, when
resistance to the drug, a large pink pill sold in the United
States under the trade name Aralen, started to show up in
Latin America and then in Asia, too. The replacement was
mefloquine hydrochloride (a large white tablet, marketed
as Lariam). Its side-effects, depending on the user, of
course, could include diarrhea, nausea, dizziness, and
headaches. This is what most of the passengers, and the
officers and crew, were taking. In the most extreme cases,
some observers have contended, the drug may also lead to
depression, hallucinations, nightmares, and panic attacks.
(Before I left Canada there was a controversy under way,
concerning the issuing of mefloquine to Canadian soldiers
performing peacekeeping duty in Somalia, where one or
more Somali prisoners were tortured and killed, igniting a
scandal that rocked the military.)

Paludrine and other drugs are in use as well, not to
mention Fansidar, which is a treatment, not a preventative.
All have potential side-effects of some sort. In the past,

when chloroquine was more useful, I found that the stuff gave me dreadful heavy-metal nightmares. With many strains of mosquito showing resistance to mefloquine, on this voyage I took doxycycline (100 milligrams a day for 115 days). Jane and Roberta were taking it as well. In my case, it brought me the most extraordinarily colourful dreams every night, colourful less in their narratives (they were rather mundane actually) than in their palette. The post-Matisse blues were particularly stunning. Later, at the end of each day, I observed a tendency towards depression, the price I paid for all the visual excitement. For one reason or another, then, few of us aboard the *Pride of Great Yarmouth* were at our best for much of the voyage.

એ

As we prepared to arrive in Papua New Guinea, the civil war that had ravaged the island of Bougainville, brought down successive governments, all but wrecked the country's economy, and led to widespread riots and even mutiny, was evidently coming to an end after nine years. The government at Port Moresby has long forbidden foreign travel to Bougainville, site of the now-closed copper mine that once accounted for 44 per cent of PNG's exports. The restrictions remained in force after the government first abandoned the island to the Bougainville Revolutionary Army and then got caught trying to send in South African mercenaries (in exchange, apparently, for rights to the mine). The rules still applied, even with a truce, peace talks, and now a multi-national peacekeeping force in place. In fact, the PNG government is paranoic about journalists and foreign observers of any kind. In order to obtain a visa, I actually had to furnish an affidavit to the effect that I am not a writer. As my contemporaries will affirm, this was more in the nature of a little white lie than an act of perjury.

Papua New Guinea is only the eastern half of the island of New Guinea, an area larger than California. The rest is the former Dutch New Guinea, now Irian Jaya, claimed by Indonesia, which has been fighting its own long counter-insurgency there. The conflict sometimes spills down the Sepik River valley into PNG. Even more so than most other places, PNG is incomprehensible to the visitor without some understanding of its history – so thick and tangled, like vines in the jungle, are its various encounters with colonialism. The role of the outsider is doubly important in this case, because very little is known about PNG before European contact. Much less has been learned in the twenty-five years since independence; archaeology and related disciplines are not fully developed in the country yet. Despite the continuing pressure to change, people today in the Highlands of PNG live the life of the tribe, each with its own language and customs (and as often as not with its own disease or genetic anomaly), different from those of neighbouring tribes, although sepa-rated perhaps by only two days' travel by foot or canoe. Almost as much as the rugged mountains that dominate a great deal of the geography of PNG, this chequerboard of distinct village cultures has ensured that, for most of modern history at least, change came from outside.

The northern and southern coasts were discovered indi-vidually, by the Portuguese, the Spanish, and the Dutch, all working against one another. In 1529, Álvaro de Saaverdra Cerón, cousin of the hated Hernán Cortés, went ashore on the northern coast, which the Portuguese had sighted three years earlier. He was the first European to meet the native population, whom he described as "black people with friz-zled hair, who are cannibals." He believed that "the Devil walks with them." A generation later, the Dutch came, and they found the people "wild, cruel black savages," especially once a Dutch landing party was killed. That was in 1605. The next year, Luis Vaez de Torres labelled them "wild and unfriendly." At all times, the feeling was mutual.

At that stage, Europeans believed that New Guinea might be a part of the fabled Australian landmass (as indeed it once had been, in a previous geological epoch). Explorers took years to fill in the map around New Guinea, showing that the Torres Strait, as it came to be called, separated Australia from New Guinea. As to the interior of New Guinea, much of it remained uncharted country until well into the twentieth century. One of the mysteries is whether the land still holds any big secrets. Many believe it does.

In 1884, the island stood divided among three European powers. As mentioned, the entire western part was Nether-lands New Guinea, now controlled by Indonesia. The other section was split between British New Guinea in the south-east and German New Guinea in the northeast. Australia was handed control of British New Guinea within a few years of Federation in 1901. Later, after the Great War, Australia was given the formerly German part to adminis-ter in trust. "Thus," writes John Dademo Waiko, historian and parliamentarian, "the fact that the people of the present-day nation of Papua New Guinea became part of the British and German colonial empires, and not the Dutch, was an accident of European history of which they had no control." As Waiko has stated, the proudest moment in the life of the present generation was when PNG proclaimed independence from Australia in 1975. The Bougainville Revolutionary Army (many of whose members have now been taken on as PNG police officers) rebelled over questions surrounding the state-controlled copper mine. Also, they felt, with some justification, that Bougainville should not be part of PNG at all but rather of the Solomon Islands, with whose culture they have most in common. The BRA never fielded more than five hundred troops, armed mostly with old shotguns and other sporting weapons. That is to say, they had no help from overseas. They did, however, enjoy the support of the local peasantry, without which they could not have survived.

Most Australians resent being labelled the former colonial masters of PNG. They were only looking after the place, they say, and it was, after all, Australian troops who fought for it so fiercely in the Second World War. But paternalism has always been a feature of colonialism (its best feature, no doubt). In any event, PNG has tended to lag since independence, both economically and politically. Partly this is the nature of the times, partly the nature of PNG, a truly troubled place. Average per capita income is US$1,249. Average daily caloric intake is only 2,609 – 1,000 fewer than in developed countries such as the United States, Canada, and France. The average life expectancy, counting female and male together, is fifty-seven years, the same as in Bangladesh; only a few countries – most of them savaged by wars and famine in recent decades – such as Nigeria, Cambodia, Laos, Afghanistan, and Bhutan, have lower figures. Population growth and inflation are both low, yet the country's foreign debt exceeds its credit balance by a factor of ten; this is clearly one of those countries held hostage by the World Bank and the International Monetary Fund. It is also a country held hostage by internal forces.

The 20,000 Australian expats in Port Moresby and other cities (down from 50,000 in the 1970s) live in fear and resignation behind security systems and razor-wire barricades. So do most other foreigners. So, in fact, do the relative handful of prosperous Papua New Guineans. Young men from villages drift into cities such as Moresby and Lae looking for work that doesn't exist. Still retaining their tribal identity, they become "rascals" (in pidgin, *raskols*), people who live by robbery. At present, they are equipped with zip guns, which use strips of inner tube and a nail to discharge 12-gauge shotgun shells. How long will it be until they have cheap knock-off automatic weapons from China? Then they may rule the daylight hours as they already rule the night. Even at the highest levels, order sometimes operates in a vacuum in PNG.

The mess in Bougainville (where Australian, New Zealand, Fijian, Tongan, and ni-Vanuatu troops now keep the peace) used up two governments. As I was writing these words, a third, the one headed by Prime Minister Bill Skate, looked a bit shaky. A videotape had surfaced in which Skate was apparently seen demanding bribes and boasting of ordering opponents murdered. At the very least, surely this made for another thorny political problem. Then there was the drought, the worst in a century, people said. Water was being rationed even in Moresby. Some villages in the interior had been reduced to eating grubs and insects, the press reported. Such was the situation into which we were sailing – through bright sun, light breezes, and day after day of ideal South Pacific weather.

Even at this late date there were changes to the fixture. The latest word was that we were not going to Indonesia after all (damn) because the copra business had suddenly picked up in PNG. How this was possible when the news was full of the devastating drought there, I didn't know. The mysteries of shipping would confound any financier I've ever heard of. We were back to the original idea of calling at Lae, on PNG's northern coast, twice rather than once. Also, we were now going to Alotau, at the tip of the narrow easternmost peninsula, as well. "Ay, now am I in Arden; the more fool I; when I was at home, I was in a better place: but travellers must be content" (*As You Like It*, II:4). Our third day out of Port Vila in Vanuatu, I watched the fiery orange sun disappear behind the outlines of Rossel Island, where a ship named the *St. Paul* was wrecked in 1858 with 326 Chinese passengers, who were eaten by the islanders. The sun slid out of sight like a happily drowning person going down for the last time. There were many other freighters on the horizon, as we had intersected the main shipping lane between Australia and the Far East.

With Alotau near, we shut down the one working engine at 0400 Sunday and drifted most of the day in order not to arrive before 0600 Monday. This way we'd once again avoid having to pay extra berthing charges. The sea was eerie in its stillness, the heat almost lethal. Two three-metre-long (ten-foot-long) sharks swam along our starboard side. The cook fed them scraps, so I supposed we'd have them as an escort for a while. They had a strange greenish tint to them, like well-oxydized copper, and were joined by an enormous barracuda. In this climate, the siesta seems a natural and inevitable practice, not some affectation or quirk of local culture. I had been asleep two and a half hours when, at 1530, a terrible rending noise yanked me awake: our one engine was starting up for the slow and dangerous run to Alotau, about 140 nautical miles away, through Milne Bay and the China Strait. This was to be our first taste of Papua New Guinea.

PNG is such an extraordinary place that almost anything one could say about it is in some measure bound to be true. It occupies half of the world's second-largest island (a distant second to Greenland). Yet the population is no more than four and a half million – Melanesians who speak at least seven hundred different languages (not dialects). The incredible ruggedness of the terrain (the description is scarcely adequate) has meant that, even today, fifty-five years after the Second World War, the American "skull squad" is still called in an average of three times a year to retrieve the remains of U.S. servicemen (fliers, mostly).

This curious little fact is not only a comment on what the war was like here but also on the nature of transportation in PNG. The latest statistic I could find was dated 1992, but it shows the country having a mere 20,000 kilometres (12,000 miles) of roads, only 618 kilometres (384 miles) of which are paved highway. Most of this second total would be accounted for by the famed Highland Highway, which begins at the coast and is fully paved as far inland as Mount Hagen or so. The highway can be travelled only in the daytime, however, and then at your own risk. Bandits. *Raskols*. Roadblocks. There are nearly 500 small airfields in use at any one time (new ones are built at approximately the same rate that old ones are reclaimed by the jungle). Yet there are only fifteen big transport aircraft in the civil fleet. Similarly, thousands of boats and ships travel the coasts and rivers, but such business is on a small scale, despite its collective enormity; the Papua New Guinea merchant marine – ships of a thousand tonnes or more – numbers but eight vessels. Astoundingly for a country where mining is so important, there are no railways. The land is simply too rough for tracks to be laid. The gold mines in the western fringes of the country near the Irian Jaya border must depend on huge Russian helicopters to take disassembled mining equipment in and out.

You won't find mention of the fact in the statistical abstracts and yearbooks, but PNG is also the world's most overly anthropologized country. Unlike Vanuatu, which has sensibly imposed a two-year moratorium on foreign academics until it can graduate enough of its own to study ni-Vanuatu culture, PNG is crawling with roving bands of anthros, mostly American but many from Australia as well, who examine the rich aboriginal landscape, as though the work of Conrad Arensberg, who shifted anthropology's focus away from primitive societies before the Second World War, never existed. Before leaving on this trip I had made a point of reading a number of the books published in the previous year or two, books with such titles as *They Make Themselves: Work and Play among the Baining of Papua New Guinea* and *The Cassowary's Revenge: The Life and Death of Masculinity in a New Guinea Society*. To be positive about it, I concluded that at best anthropology is a higher and more well-meaning discipline than, say, sociology, which occupies the same place in the humanities that Human

Resources does in business and Policy does in government: hocus-pocus, essentially pornographic.

Anthropologists and others would have you believe that the best time to visit PNG is always yesterday, before it was exposed to western daylight. True, the first Papua New Guinean I saw, when I awoke to find us tying up at Alotau, was paddling a dugout canoe round the ship while talking on a cellular phone. In the 1920s, the Leahy brothers from Australia – gold prospectors, and the New Guinea equivalent of Wyatt, Virgil, and Morgan Earp – found so-called Stone Age people in the Mount Hagen area who had no previous experience of Europeans. Others insist that "the last hidden valley" and its primitive human treasures were opened up only as late as 1977, once the Highland Highway reached places as far distant as Tari, near the absolute centre of the country, or indeed in 1993, when someone stumbled on a tribe called the Liawep, seventy-nine strong. Some contend that there are still villages no European has ever seen. Still others insist that ritual cannibalism was practised in some areas as late as the 1960s or even more recently. Such Margaret Mead–ism is doubtless a disservice to Papua New Guineans (34 per cent of whom, however, still follow indigenous belief systems, as opposed to the 22 per cent who adhere to Catholicism or the 16 per cent who are Lutherans – these last, a reminiscence of the German presence that was once so strong in the north). In my view, western attention would be put to better use improving health care than extracting thesis material from tribal ways in the same manner that palm oil is squeezed out of palm nuts. Trained dentists and even X-ray technicians are difficult to locate in PNG; apparently they're not as much fun to look for as recidivist cannibals.

PNG, a land of beauty and woe, has more than one hundred volcanoes, thirty-eight of them still capable of eruption; hot springs and endless caves; frequent earthquakes; flame trees and three-metre-tall Highland poinsettias; cockatoos and birds of paradise. Because New Guinea was once linked by a land bridge to Australia, it is also home to the bandicoot and the tree-climbing kangaroo. It is a place of strange creatures of the sea as well as the land and air: shark-eating whales, for example. There are also strange (to us) peoples and practices, such as the famous wigmen and mud-warriors, so called, obviously, for the ways they decorate themselves, preparing for the rituals for which Papua New Guineans are so avid. There are places where men catch needlefish using nets made of gigantic spiders' webs; and subsistence agriculture (sweet potatoes, taro, breadfruit, pineapples, bananas, and much more) remains the livelihood of 85 per cent of the population.

For most people, life is still centred in the village. In turn, village life is measured in traditions and customs as different as the *singsong* (self-explanatory) and *payback* (the system for settling affronts to honour by extortion, compensation, and dowries). Being poor in material goods, the people are rich in imagination. They use what they possess to every conceivable advantage. The list of what they can do with the sago palm is extraordinary. Likewise the pandanus tree, which provides thatched roofs and the strings on which seashell beads are strung. Much of the activity I describe takes place in surroundings of an almost unimaginable natural hostility, including the great river systems of the Sepik and the Fly. In the Second World War, Japan sent 100,000 troops into the Sepik region; only 13,000 survived the conditions there – the malaria and other diseases and all the traps that nature had laid for them (and for the Allies).

Our point of entry into this strange and dangerous land was Alotau, the capital of Milne Bay, the most southeasterly of PNG's twenty provinces, at the end of the long peninsula that has Port Moresby on one side, facing the Coral Sea, and Lae, the second-most-important city, on the other, facing the Solomon Sea. Alotau is isolated from both. It is a poky little frontier town, surrounded on three sides by grown-over volcanic peaks, their origin betrayed by their razor-like edges and unexpected declivities, and on the fourth by Milne Bay. The town has two streets, each one long block in length, along which are the customary South Pacific stores, Chinese and otherwise, and groups of angry-looking unemployed males blocking access to elevated foot-paths. This is a place where everyone who can afford to be is armed. So is everyone who can't afford not to be.

A short distance from the town site, through a mangrove swamp and past a permanent fire for smoking fish, stands the market. It houses a few pathetic rows of wooden stalls, where country people sell fruits and tubers and betel nut, the mild narcotic many chew habitually, turning their teeth (and their spit) as red as lipstick. Some stalls offer small packets of powdered coral lime, which, if taken with betel nut, is supposed to kill the taste of the stuff (though people are prepared to tolerate its downside to take the edge off their sometimes wretched lives). This was the first public market I'd ever seen anywhere in the world that was sur-rounded by a cyclone fence topped with barbed wire and had a sentry to frisk everyone who enters. Such security rather defeats the civic purpose of a public market. Not at all what the Greeks had in mind. And this is only a subtle hint of how far-reaching the crime problem is.

For the *Pride of Great Yarmouth*, whose arrival was a major economic event in the town, Alotau is a good if tricky port, though we were reaching it at a bad time. We had nothing to discharge and only a load of palm oil to take on. Palm oil was a prudent cargo for us, because its value is high relative to its volume (about thirty American cents a pound – it is always measured by the pound, for some reason), and also because it requires no stevedoring. The liquid had been collected from small producers in a huge underground storage tank, and it was pumped directly into one of our holds through a ten-inch hose, as though we were a small craft buying fuel at the British Petroleum wharf found in every Pacific port. Nothing could be easier.

I was looking over the port rail with Roberta, the Scotswoman, and Jane, her Yorkshire friend, when the captain brought the ship in without a pilot (a pilot is optional in this harbour). The town itself is first hidden by thick vegetation so that we saw only scattered houses, some thatched and others with roofing of the ubiquitous corrugated-iron sheeting. This is held in place with rocks, making it easier to replace after each typhoon. All the dwellings had small garden plots; the soil was rich and red. As in Vila, the harbour is like a tropical aquarium, buzzing with tiger-fish.

The agent walked up to the dock in a white blouse and black skirt, but carrying her shoes tied round her neck; apparently, though she goes barefoot as a rule, she did not feel that this would be proper when calling on a client vessel. There was a strongly made godown on the dockside. A bit farther along was a jetty where the small inter-island traders and coasters tie up. People were sitting on the beach with their possessions in cardboard cartons or in bilums, the traditional string carryalls of PNG, awaiting their chance to board a ship that was unloading deck cargo of colourfully painted 200-litre drums. Dugouts were circling our ship, making complete circuits by ducking under part of the raised dock. Wood smoke hovered in the air from the massive forest fires in the region, and the mountaintops were lost in haze, the result of El Niño. So humid was it here on the coast that it seemed incredible that the Australian military was operating such a large-scale airlift for people in the Highlands, where some 900,000 were withering because of the lack of rainfall.

I returned to my cabin to get the little haversack I carried with me ashore – disposable camera, first-aid kit, pencil and paper, Swiss army knife – and began to make my way along the red dusty road to town. One otherwise quite ordinary-looking Papuan (most people in PNG wear secondhand clothing, which is imported as a commodity in unsorted lots) suddenly produced a bird of paradise feather from inside his shirt to flag a taxi, or rather a small flat-bed truck with wooden benches in the back and the word *TAXI* hand-painted on the doors. Hitching into town together (for we had been warned to travel in groups even during the day), Roberta, Jane, the doctor, the doctor's wife, and I – the British contingent with me representing the entire Commonwealth – saw two types of wildlife in abundance: rats and butterflies. Some of the latter are large, bright-blue fellows with black trim – the *Papua ulysses*, I believe, also found in the Solomon Islands, where people hunt them for profit (specimens can bring US$150 retail in London).

We wandered through the few shops, finding them poorly stocked, with goods that were both expensive and shoddy.

"This is what the old frontier towns must have been like," I said. "Nobody makes eye contact with anyone else for fear of starting a fight." Many of the toughs who were sprawled out in little patches of shade carried broomsticks and machetes, the tools used in combination to reap tall grasses.

We had heard that there was a pub in town, or rather a short distance the other side of town. Actually it was an Australian expats' club, the kind with dart boards and point-of-sale advertising for Foster's. The world of the Aussies in PNG is one into which I now have more insight from reading the wonderfully comic fiction of Michael Challinger, the author of *Port Moresby Mixed Doubles* and other works. When we located the club, we found it protected by fierce dogs and barbed wire. Were it not for the drought, the jungle would have long ago reclaimed the rugby field, which lay instead like a brown square of desert scrub set down in the wrong landscape. Across the harbour, we saw activity of sorts aboard the *Pride of Great Yarmouth*, which dwarfed the town. Thick smoke, black and oily, was rising maybe 15 metres (50 feet) from one of the funnels and being carried towards the already-polluted community by an all-too-brief offshore breeze. It looked like a large balloon in a comic strip – the space where the ship's thoughts should have been written out. We had accumulated a great deal of rubbish since before Vanuatu. It was now being burned in the incinerator, one piece of the ship's equipment that was still functioning as it was designed to do.

8

PAPUA NEW GUINEA:

VOLCANOES AND *RASKOLS*

*D*EPARTING ALOTAU, we sailed coastwise all day and night, never out of sight of land on the port side, while the pall of smoke and haze thickened and kept everyone off the deck. Before we left Alotau, we had been joined by three fitters, Singaporean Chinese engineers, who were to install the new wheel for the Number One engine. The part itself had not arrived. In the meantime, they had discovered another problem. The camshaft had twisted a bit in the few seconds that the engine had been running with a broken gear. Everything was thrown out of alignment, and the flywheel and the two banks of fuel pumps had to be taken apart. By actual measurement, the temperature in the engine room reached forty-two degrees Celsius. People can work in such heat, in such a tight space, only fifteen minutes at a time.

It seems incredible that Lae should claim to have 85,000 people; though its residential sections are spread over a wide plain between the shore and the foot of the volcanoes, the actual townsite is minute, a ragtag collection of dusty small businesses and a single decent hotel. At one end of town is an abandoned airfield – abandoned but still home to the offices of Air Nuigini and other companies, which have yet to make the transition to the new airport outside the city. The old one, slowly being reclaimed by the vegetation, is the place from which Amelia Earhart disappeared. She took off in her Lockheed Electra in 1937, en route to Howland Island, Hawaii, and Oakland, California, on the last lap of her attempt to become the first woman to fly round the world, and was never heard from again. The history of PNG, where aviation was and remains the main form of transport, is rich in such incidents. In North Solomons Province, one can visit the wreckage of Admiral Isoroku Yamamoto's aircraft. Yamamoto (1884–1943) masterminded Japan's attack on Pearl Harbor. He took off from Rabaul, not knowing that the Americans had penetrated the Japanese code and knew his flight plan.

No one could count all the barbed and concertina wire used in Lae, where security is the most important growth sector. Uniformed security frisk all non-Europeans leaving the supermarkets; other rent-a-cops work as clerks in small shops, being the only people allowed near the tills. Each bus requires a guard sitting next to the driver. Only the absence of advanced technology prevents the city from taking on an Orwellian or Kafkaesque quality. Instead, Lae simply seems, as a previous observer said, a Third World city with all the associated problems and none of the compensating charms – no interesting architecture, no traces of a colonial past, no colourful street life, or indeed street life of any kind except violence, which is random and virtually omnipresent. The city's only obvious cultural asset, aside from the harbour view, is the Botanical Gardens, which foreigners are now advised to avoid, even in daylight, even in groups. Our shipping company's South Pacific supervisor, an Australian and a former merchant captain himself, said that he had had enough. He was moving his family back to Oz. Faxes and e-mail now make it possible for him to do his job without the danger of living in Lae.

We were in Lae to off-load containers in order to gain access to the forward starboard hold, which we would fill with copra at ports in New Britain Province to the north; we would pick up the containers on the way back and stack them in their old spot. This stop at Lae, then, was profitable only in terms of a larger picture, not as a port of call in its own right. The supervisor had been able to brighten the outlook somewhat, however, by locating a customer who needed vehicles shipped along the coast to Madang: an easy ro-ro job.

The new gear wheel had indeed made its way from Britain to Port Moresby, and the engine was stripped down and ready to receive it. But the damned part was not able to find passage on any aircraft leaving the capital for Lae. Plan B kicked in with the effect of an emergency generator. Some brave soul would begin to drive the thing by truck the whole rugged way from Moresby to Madang, or as far as he could, along what might charitably be called unimproved roads. Meanwhile, the trio from Singapore were enjoying the hospitality of our galley and spare cabins. I overheard one of the officers (I won't identify him further) say, "Jesus Christ, twenty-five years ago you'd only hire a Singapore Chinese to be your *amah* or houseman. Now we're flying them in as engineers." I was embarrassed, and walked away. I never know how else to respond to racist statements like that.

Lae wasn't made any more attractive by hours of rain. "It's just coastal rain," the agent said. "Ten miles inland and they're still eating bugs to survive the drought."

He had come aboard to deliver mail, provisions, and a bit of news. The *Pride of Bournemouth*, our sister ship, which had been laid up at Panama City with generator trouble, had finally got its light plant replaced and had made its way to Papeete, only to discover that its bunkers were tainted.

"Sometimes good-quality oil will get contaminated with organisms that live on the additives," an engineer explained. "But nothing can live in fuel oil, which is basically pretty generic stuff, what's left over at the refinery. Of course, it could get contaminated by water, but that's easily skimmed off. That's why a ship has purifiers. The problem must be chemicals that have leaked into the fuel somehow."

So the *Pride of Bournemouth* was going to Auckland to have all its bunkers pumped out, at the rate of twenty tonnes an hour; the contents would be disposed of safely, and the bunkers cleaned and then refilled. How would this affect the *Pride of Great Yarmouth*? There were two differing opinions. One held that the *Bournemouth*, having both its engines, unlike us, should make up for lost time and resume its place in the rotation, relieving us of the added pressure to take on as much as we could as quickly as we could and come through with a voyage in the black (notwithstanding such unbudgeted expenses as the team of Singaporeans being paid by the hour to gorge themselves on our food-stuffs). The opposing view was that the distance between the two ships would now be shorter, freeing us to get to Europe faster with what we had already taken aboard, leaving the *Bournemouth* to sweep up all the copra, cocoa, coffee, and palm oil we had missed, or would miss. But these were simply guesses.

We were, after all, tramping-trawling for commerce. The officers weren't really in possession of a detailed map of the future; certainly few facts filtered down to us passengers. We simply had to settle back, find our own sources of content-ment and fulfil our own needs, independent of the occult world of economics. At about suppertime on this day, with the containers where they should be and the ro-ro (second-hand Japanese trucks) driven aboard, we got under way for Madang, population about 25,000, the seat of Madang Province, about as far from Lae as Lae was from Alotau. We would arrive the next afternoon. The engineers from Singapore, one of whom had a grey ponytail (who does he think he is, the bosun?) were digging into roast beef and Yorkshire pudding. Over their heads, the engine-room alarm light was twitching on and off as the old analog bell sounded. Everyone was oblivious.

The gear that had been flown 9,500 miles or so from London to Port Moresby, and then somehow hauled through bandit country to Madang, turned out to be the wrong size. The three wise men from Singapore went back to sitting on their haunches, as the captain and a worried-looking chief engineer walked into town in the hope of finding a tele-phone box from which to call Britain, the ship's own over-seas communications system having broken down again. I met them walking the other way, after a lingering excur-sion through this picturesque city – far more attractive in every way than the much larger Lae, for example.

The town is approached through a grab-bag of islands, some large, others just a few hectares, with the biggest one, Kranket, on the starboard side of the Dallman Passage as we entered; a ferry connects it with the mainland. In Madang Province, just as in Milne Bay Province, there was little sign of the horrible drought that was causing such misery in the interior, though through my binoculars I believed I could see some evidence in the piebald pattern of the second or third range of mountains. The weekend edition of the national newspaper, the *Post-Courier* (circulation 36,000), ran an amazing photograph of two deep-water freighters left high and dry in the Fly River estuary as the water level dropped from more than 11 metres (36 feet) to only 0.2 metres (8 inches). The *Post-Courier*, by the way, states proudly on its masthead that 29.5 per cent of Papua New Guineans indirectly own shares in the paper through pension schemes or unions (there are twenty-some labour unions in PNG, the same number as there are political parties). The fact that the rest is controlled by Rupert Murdoch is glossed over.

The upper-middle class of Madang is more conspicuous than its opposite numbers in the other parts of PNG I had seen, or soon expected to see. Madang doesn't seem to have resolved itself along class lines, not geographically at least. The homes of the well-off, with their satellite dishes and private piers, share the shoreline with modest places that have outhouses perched out over the surf. Madang also seems cleaner and more orderly than the other spots we had visited in this part of the world. One is tempted to put this down to the German influence, for this was the capital of the old German colony and headquarters of the New Guinea Compagnie. A main feature of the city centre, which finds its focus in an intersection dotted with mostly Australian banks, is a cemetery with German inscriptions on many of the headstones. *"Hier ruhen Herr Karl Buschat am. 10. Febr. 1861 auf Memel / am 10 Marz 1908 und dessen Ehefrau Friederike Louise Anna geb. Kohlenberg..."* The rest is worn away. Or *"Hier ruht in Gott KARL MÖDER 7.3.1914."* These and the others were doubtless victims of malaria, which hit the Germans with particular force (in retribution, some have suggested, for the terror of their rule, which the New Guineans found much harsher than that of the British or the Dutch).

Perhaps the most unusual feature of Madang, however, is its bat population, which numbers in the tens of thousands, it seemed to me. The creatures hang upside down, as bats will, from the high branches of huge old banyan trees that punctuate the principal thoroughfares. They seem somehow like British commuters waiting for a train, with newspapers folded neatly under their arms. Then one or two will begin to squeal, a noise that sounds like the conversation of mice run through powerful amplifiers (for they are mice of a kind). The others join in, and suddenly you can't hear your own thoughts. The bats are an important community asset, as they feed on mosquitoes – mozzies, the Australian term, is the preferred usage here – and big red ants.

Many north-central tribal people come to Madang with crafts to sell to dealers and market operators, particularly these days, when yams, their staple crop, have been hit hard by the bad weather. It's extraordinary to see faces and bodies covered with decorative tattoos and know that these people are not folk entertainers or some sort of living exhibit, just ordinary people who happen to be in town from some village. The design and the craftsmanship of their wares are both of a high level. Particularly clever and well made are the bilums, many of them brightly coloured and others woven of what looks like undyed burlap. They are carried by both men and women, though women are as likely to carry the strap across their foreheads as on their shoulders. Significantly, the city- and town-dwelling Papua New Guineans don't seem to fancy bilums the way village people do, preferring western-style backpacks, to prove that they aren't bumpkins. Thus do cultures decay.

Madang in any case is certainly a place where customs and people meet. It was the first place where, as we steamed into the harbour, locals took photographs of *us*, in our strange and colourful European attire. The berthing would have been difficult even with two working engines to play off against each other in coming alongside the wharf. Our captain executed one of the neatest jobs of parallel parking I've ever seen, slipping the *Pride of Great Yarmouth* into a space that looked too tight for it, then kedging us in a bit with hawsers.

We remained no longer than we had to. Another freighter – *Asian Prosperity* was its name – was queued up for our berth, so the dockers worked until midnight the first evening (at Sunday wages) and all the following day, loading 1,700 tonnes of copra. Before we departed, I learned that the three engineers from Singapore were going back home. This would probably mean that somebody would try to have the correct gear waiting for us at Rabaul, our next port, or at Singapore. And that we would do the work ourselves. Failing that, and factoring in further complications, a delay on the transit to Antwerp seemed inevitable.

One more thing: when I went for a walk around the ship, I discovered that enormous brown moths, the size of paper-back novels, were sunning themselves on the top deck, lined up in rows, wing to wing. I must confess that I do not understand the lepidopterous mind.

～

Rabaul, a community on the northern coast of East New Britain Province, northeast of the PNG mainland in the Bismarck Sea, is an odd and eerie place whose population cannot be judged accurately. The figure was about 15,000 in 1993, the year before most of the town was destroyed in the biggest, but by no means the most recent, of a series of devastating volcanic eruptions. Four active volcanoes, called Mother, North Daughter, South Daughter, and Vulcan, ring Simpson Harbour, which is considered one of the finest and (insofar as weather is concerned) safest anchor-ages in the Pacific. This reputation exists despite the fact that the harbour, Karavia Bay, and indeed the whole Gazelle Peninsula of which they are part, are littered with an enor-mous amount of debris from four years' fighting during the Second World War. At least fifty Japanese wrecks lie on the bottom, put there by the American, Australian, and New Zealand air forces as the payback for Pearl Harbor and as a precaution against a Japanese advance from New Guinea into Australia. The ships have names such as *Hakkai Maru* and *Kenshin Maru*, two of five freighters sunk in one day by bombers based on Bougainville. Two months later, at least another eight went down in a single raid, part of Operation Cartwheel. A merchant ship called the *Komaki Maru* had earlier, in 1942, been sunk at the main berth. It is still there; filled with concrete, it's now used as a wharf. The *Pride of Great Yarmouth* was tied up next to it, taking on a load of coffee in 72-kilogram (160-pound) burlap bags, and also some cocoa.

No rain had fallen in Rabaul for six months. In general, places on the coast had been spared the full effects of the great drought experienced by the heavily populated Highlands and westernmost provinces. That Rabaul should be the striking exception is altogether in character with its reputation as a hard-luck kind of town. The bad fortune, in fact, predates the town itself. Philip Carteret describes an eruption he witnessed from HMS *Swallow* in 1767. The next major one came in 1791 on Tavurvur, on the eastern side of the ring; its other notable eruptions were in 1878–79. In the past three years, a number of local residents have been buried alive in the loose volcanic dust of Tavurvur while hunting for megapode eggs, a local delicacy.

The worst disaster took place in 1937 when five hundred people were killed. In his classic memoir, *Navigation in the South Seas*, Brett Hilder, who sailed on Burns Philp ships for forty-two years, about half of the total time that this historic company (which was fighting bankruptcy as I was writing this) maintained its own fleet. In 1937, he writes, on only his second voyage on the company's *Montoro*:

> we were lying at the wharf in Rabaul, discharging cargo in the humid heat and surrounded by the circle of dead, dormant and steaming volcanoes. At mid-day we were sitting on deck having our lunch, when a violent 'quake shook the ship and rattled the plates and the table. Rabaul is noted for its shakes, locally known by the native name

guria. This last shake was one of a series which had been getting worse daily, but as there hadn't been an eruption for nearly sixty years, there was no undue alarm. The sea-level fell several feet and rose again like a flood tide or bore and it was reported that some reefs near the entrance had risen a few feet and were now nearly awash. We left Rabaul that afternoon for our next port, Kavieng [on New Ireland, just north of New Britain], and had just left that port the following day when we got our first news of the eruption. This included an S.O.S. for us to return to Rabaul to help evacuate the town.

By midnight, when I came on watch, it was bright moonlight, in fact everything seemed to be whiter than usual. I soon found that this was due to a fine white dust carried by the wind, the south east trade, over one hundred and fifty miles from the eruption at Rabaul.

The heavier dirt, ashes, pumice and rocks were falling on the area around Rabaul from a brand new volcano. This had arisen on the site of a low muddy island near the harbour entrance and called Vulcan Island by the Germans [who had first colonized Rabaul] because of the hot springs. Between the island and the shore was a sheltered little strait, and a local firm had built a slipway nearby to take ships up to five hundred tons. One of these ships, S.S. *Durour*, was up on the slip for overhaul and, this being completed, the crew were standing by to get back into the water. The violent shakes were ringing the ship's bell continuously and had shaken all the props and ladders away from the ship's sides. The crew could hardly be blamed for going over the side down ropes. . . . They had just left the ship in time, for Vulcan Island gave a couple of convulsive heaves, then blew straight up into the sky like the cork from a champagne bottle.

The column of smoke, steam, hot ash and black mud went to a height of about six miles. . . . Red hot rocks, up to the size of motor cars and small cottages, fell at intervals. . . . The new volcano built itself up to six hundred feet in the first twenty-four hours, as well as joining Vulcan

Island to the mainland. . . . During the first terrible night the main road nearby was buried under forty feet of pumice, so that the few European homes were completely covered and hundreds of natives were buried in the villages. Next morning did not dawn in the town of Rabaul, for the dense pall of ash kept the area in darkness and provided a steady shower of pumice and stone.

Today some of the other volcanoes dwarf Vulcan, which, because of later tantrums, is now as much a crater as it is a mountain. When the Japanese staged an amphibious invasion of Rabaul, however, Vulcan was still the highest eminence. Accordingly, it was fortified by the invaders, who came to town in January 1942 to make Rabaul their base from which to attack Port Moresby and, eventually, they hoped, effect a landing in Australia. At that time, Tavurvur was erupting periodically, and would continue to do so through much of 1943. By then, the tide had turned against the Japanese following Coral Sea and Bismarck Sea, both great naval battles but fought in the air by carrier-based planes. The Japanese, however, continued to cling tenaciously to Rabaul, with many miles of secret tunnels in the hills and mountains, dug using local slave labour, and caverns large enough to be used by barges and, in one case, by submarines. The Europeans, those not killed outright in the fighting, were put aboard the *Montevideo Maru* for shipment to Japan. An American sub-marine, unaware of the nature of the cargo, torpedoed the ship off Luzon. All perished. Rabaul and New Guinea in general were in fierce contention during the war. Foreign soldiers outnumbered the indigenous population two to one: 1 million Americans, 250,000 Australians, and 300,000

Japanese. Of this last group, two-thirds were killed. Very few surrendered.

Postwar Rabaul began to prosper. Relations between the Papua New Guineans and the foreigners, mostly Australians and Americans, were never again as they had been before the war. The Melanesians had been invaded by friendly forces as well as the Japanese, and this left them with an appetite for foreign prosperity. The 1950s and 1960s were a productive time of growth, but in the 1970s Rabaul's volcanoes began to seethe again. The disaster that everyone knew would arrive one day gave no warning when it finally unleashed its devastation. In September 1994, two volcanoes erupted simultaneously, causing a total black-out and creating an impenetrable pumice raft that floated on the beautiful harbour for five weeks. The clean-up was not yet complete when Rabaul was administered the coup de grace, in April 1995. Except for the harbour facilities, everything in a 2-kilometre (1.2-mile) radius was pretty much destroyed. Only five people were killed this time, while steam and lava shot 30 kilometres (18 miles) high, the former disappearing into the atmosphere, the latter layering the earth 2 metres deep (6.5 feet). Pyroclastic flames and tidal waves added to the destruction. If surrounding villages are taken into account, about 90,000 Papua New Guineans were displaced. There was another lesser eruption in 1996. As it happens, the *Pride of Great Yarmouth* had been present for that one, and had to make a run for open water.

Perhaps the biggest of PNG's social problems today is crime committed by young people with no other means of livelihood. At first, *raskols* were confined largely to Port Moresby, the capital city to which so many tribal people drifted, seeking work but ending up in shantytowns. Gangs occupied and controlled whole districts. Then the menace spread to Lae and also Madang and other urban areas, until it became a phenomenon of the city and the bush equally, inextricably bound up with allegiance to one's native village and, through that, to a particular clan. In the cities or the wild, along the coasts or in the interior, the situation is now virtually the same: because the same economic conditions obtain everywhere. Rascalism would seem to be both a symbol and an inevitable symptom of PNG's politics since independence in 1975 – the conflicting impulses of nationalist pride and tribal primacy. In colonial days, whites called the Melanesians "natives." After independence, the favoured term was "nationals." Now that usage is in disfavour. One is supposed to speak of a Papua New Guinean as "a Tolai from Rabaul" or "a Huli from the Highlands" or whatever the case may be.

Even from a great distance out at sea, we could observe that something was not quite right about Rabaul. Two of the volcanoes were steaming. The hills behind the town, which should have been green and jungly, were brown and bare. One of the mounds exhibited huge lunar-type craters on its face. Clouds passing overhead gave the whole scene a mottled effect that added to the strangeness.

As we entered the harbour, which was full of jellyfish with their stingers at the ready, we saw the usual landmarks of a Pacific port: the BP wharf, the Coca-Cola bottling plant. Then on the starboard side we passed the Rabaul airport, which was abandoned in 1995 and never reclaimed. The dock area was busy. An inter-island vessel was about to depart for the New Ireland coast, and hordes of people were queued up to take deck passage, complete with their huge parcels and extended families. But we perceived that the activity, or activity of any kind, extended back only 100 metres (110 yards) or so from where the water lapped at the wharves. Beyond that, Rabaul is a ghost town.

Even today, people sometimes find unexploded Japanese artillery shells in Rabaul. I saw that several examples (defused, I hoped) had been set upright in concrete for use as bollards, in somewhat the same way that London is full of hitching posts made from cannon suddenly superfluous at the close of the Napoleonic Wars. Near the sunken Japanese freighter that locals call the ship-wharf, I found that a *raskol* gang had taken up residence in abandoned shipping containers. Beyond that was the former main street, obviously a stately boulevard in its day, with patrician trees in the traffic island running down the centre. Now it lay deserted, and the trees dead or dying. Shopping plazas, large stores, office blocks, shop-fronts, dwellings – all were vacant shells. The streets and the air were thick with volcanic dust, dark grey in colour and the consistency of talcum powder, containing a high percentage of grit that gets into one's hair, eyes, ears, nostrils. In the derelict buildings, many of which showed evidence of fire, wind has swept the stuff into deep drifts in the corners.

Volcanologists, at least one of whom is killed on the job somewhere in the world each year, are becoming increasingly sophisticated about predicting eruptions. The people of Montserrat, the British colony in the Caribbean, had recently lost much of their property, but their lives were spared. This was in contrast with Mount Unzen in Japan, where about forty people were killed in 1991, or Mount

Saint Helens in the U.S. Pacific Northwest where, despite the remoteness of the site, casualties were part of the tragedy there in 1980. As well as improving volcano prediction (and simulation), science is also emphasizing that volcanoes ain't all bad. The constant pushing-up towards the surface of stuff from far down inside the Earth replenishes the supply of accessible gold, diamonds, and other valuable commodities. Past volcanoes provide palaeontologists with many of the fossils they study and especially enrich the soil in some of the world's wine-making and coffee-growing regions. The Romans knew the advantages of using volcanic debris in road-building. Obsidian, the volcanic glass so highly valued among early Native Americans as an object of trade, is used today in eye surgeons' instruments. There is even a trace of volcanic material in some kinds of toothpaste. Volcanic clay is the basis of kitty-litter. And so on.

Volcanic spectacles have always held fatal and near-fatal attractions for observers. Pliny the Elder died in the eruption of Vesuvius in 79 CE. The same volcano nearly claimed the life of Goethe in 1787. "We tried to go half a dozen steps further," Goethe wrote, "but the ground under our feet became hotter and hotter and a whirl of dense fumes darkened the sun and almost suffocated us."

Yet the bright side of volcanoes seemed impossibly remote in Rabaul. In three years, little rebuilding had been done. Partly this could be traced to the economic downturn in PNG, a trend that seemed to have little to do with anything that the outside world could prevent, particularly after almost a decade of fighting on Bougainville. There's nothing like a civil war, however small, to frighten away investment.

I walked for what seemed an eternity through the post-apocalyptic landscape, until I found a shop open – a temporary post office, set up in a deserted gasoline station, where the postmistress had been joined by a man selling small quantities of emergency supplies such as candles, kerosene, and tins of corned beef. The *bung*, or market, wiped out in the catastrophe, is slowly coming back to life on the other side of town, far from its old site (and its former central role). Most stirrings now take place at a spot about a half-hour's drive from Rabaul itself. That's how far one must travel for any but the barest of bare necessities. Rabaul may claim to still be home to 2,000 people, but I have to suspect the statement is no more than civic boosterism. When a town is dying, talk is always the last thing to go.

∾

The ship was on fire. No, that's an exaggeration. Some of the cargo was on fire. We were in the port of Kimbe, taking on copra in the Number One hold when black oily smoke, pungent and sickening, began seeping out of Number Three. The Russian bosun, hurrying to the scene, said to us sternly, "It is forbidden to be frightened." Nonetheless, the sight of the sky filling up with smoke clearly coming from inside the *Pride of Great Yarmouth* caused a tremendous hubbub. We passengers ran up to the monkey deck to get out of the way, and also to get a better view of the action. While I couldn't make out everything being said amid the commotion on the cargo deck far below, I could interpret the pantomime.

The lower reaches of Number Three had been filled with copra back in Santo, more than a fortnight earlier, over a two-day period with intermittent rain. This meant that the hatch had had to be opened and closed a number of times, and that the stevedores periodically ran for cover. What happened, I am sure, was that, despite everyone's best efforts, some of the stuff was loaded wet or got wet once it was in the hold, whereupon more was piled on top, leaving the wet layer to grow slowly hotter and hotter, like a good-tempered person finally provoked beyond endurance. It had taken that long for the heat to manifest itself as fire.

"Do you think we should go stand by our lifeboat stations?" asked Jane, the English nurse.

"I doubt that will be necessary," the doctor replied.

Tim added, "We're tied up at the wharf!"

"Still, they could tell us to abandon, couldn't they?" Roberta wanted to know.

"I suppose," the doctor answered. "But the gangplank is down. Surely we'd simply walk."

The fumes were choking our speech and making our eyes burn by this time. The others decided to go wait in the passenger lounge, which was the designated assembly point in the event of trouble. I stayed to see what would happen, but moved upwind.

You can't put out a copra fire with water, for water causes the fire in the first place. I watched to see what the protocol, then, was. Everyone and his uncle had now entered the debate down below, and I could sense two conflicting points of view wafting my way. One was to keep the hatch closed and indeed seal all the cracks and closures, depriving the fire of the oxygen it would need to continue. No one knew how long it would take the fire to burn itself out, or in fact how long it had been burning already, undetected by the sensors or our noses. And then, the question was how much of the cargo would be lost. The opposing view called for opening the hatch, which might cause the fire to suddenly jump at the same time that it allowed for an assessment of how bad the situation might be and how best to handle it. Eventually, a compromise was agreed upon. They opened the hatch halfway. Sure enough, the whole atmosphere seemed to turn black, even though no flames were visible. Then a brave crew of seamen jumped down into the hold with bloody big hoses connected to tanks of CO_2 and laid down a very thick layer of the stuff atop the copra, as though they were spreading icing on some monstrous birthday cake. The men then retreated, the hatch was closed and sealed. Gauges would eventually show the temperature within slowly dropping back to normal levels. The crisis was averted. The cargo was saved. The day, however, was pretty much shot.

Kimbe seemed an odd little place, a small blister on the map. A tanker from Rabaul had beaten us there. Since there was only one berth (Kimbe is indeed a one-berth town), we spent all the first afternoon and night at anchor about 3.2 kilometres (2 miles) out. On its last voyage, the ship was stuck at Kimbe for a record thirteen days, and no one was eager to have this happen again. Put it this way: Kimbe would seem, to South Pacific mariners, as Wawa, Ontario, is to hitchhikers on the Trans-Canada Highway. On our first day there was also an announcement over the intercom about a whale-sighting to starboard. And, the *second* new gear arrived from Port Moresby. It would be installed by the engineers who were part of the normal ship's company, without external assistance.

There was one hotel in Kimbe, right outside the wharf gate. Security thugs sat on the crumbling front steps. Inside, I found iron bars, bulletproof glass, and a sign stating that all accommodation was payable in advance, cash only. The joint was run by a tough Aussie, who was confined to a wheelchair and carried all the room keys on a noisy ring on his belt. There was a casino off the lobby with a sign saying, "Management orders. No bare feet. No gamblers under 18. No chewing buai."

The main part of town, a short walk along a dusty highway, had the usual square block of Chinese and other stores, including an extremely general store, where the stock on display featured, among other wares, coffins, with mother-of-pearl crucifixes on the lids. At 595 *kinas*, they are not cheap, but then one's loved ones deserve only the best. (I was relieved to find no coffin in my size – 42 Tall.) A large park, full of weeds and scrub, and then the markethouse, with its now-familiar security procedures and piteous stunted vegetables, completed the picture. Probably a thousand people were in town, as it was payday – a very dangerous time. Having got their pay packets, discharged their debts, and completed their shopping, men were sitting on one of the lofty pavements, spitting betel juice at the passing Europeans (a small handful of us) and waiting for some interesting trouble to break out.

Every retail house in town sold galvanized metal strong-boxes, with big hasps to accommodate stout locks; the boxes come in all sizes, according to one's wealth, and are found everywhere in PNG. While I was at the markethouse,

I actually saw a man pay for food with shell money. I was told that he was probably from New Ireland, and had come into Kimbe because of the drought. In PNG's newspapers (none of which is for sale in Kimbe, apparently) one sometimes reads a bit of nonsense by some politician about how Port Moresby must move quickly to become an important offshore banking and financial centre. Yet in Kimbe, not far away as the crow flies, I observed the dealings of someone who still lives in the age of wampum. Wonderful.

The tension in the place was beginning to give me the heebie-jeebies, and I was glad when all the copra was aboard with the local palm oil we were also taking on. I observed that in Kimbe the spillage that results from loading copra was simply left to decompose and disappear; in Luganville, by contrast, the right to sweep up any fallen bits of copra is sold or auctioned to a local person, who, over the course of one season, is able to assemble a small pile of copra bags for sale through the local marketing board. Leaving Kimbe (we actually had to wait for the high tide), we passed a large school of dolphins.

We were on our way back to Lae, where we would pick up the containers that we had stowed on our first call. Some of them were of the ventilated type, and they, I discovered, had been filled with coffee beans in our absence: more cargo for Europe. In Lae we heard other good news. The on-again–off-again call at Indonesia was on again; we would be arriving in Bandar Lampung in little more than a week. With this in mind, I hiked through Lae one more time to sell my PNG *kinas* and buy some Indonesian *rupiahs*. There is not a great deal of trade or travel between these two countries, and I soon exhausted the supply of all the banks and bureaux de change in my search. Emerging from one bank, I saw an armoured car pull up. Its windshield, and one side panel, were riddled with bullet-holes. They looked relatively fresh. The guards delivering cash to the bank branch carried shields as well as guns and wore riot helmets.

The next day, en route to Bandar Lampung, still with only one engine, was our eighty-first at sea. Eighty-one days without a serious act of mutiny or a single indictable case of passenger homicide. We saw the sun set over a volcano on the port side. The glow imparted a sparkle to all the dust in the air. At noon the day after, we were off the vexed Irian Jaya–PNG border. Our eighty-second day would end in a scarlet and orange sunset, and another row at the dinner table between the different nationalities.

9

BANDAR, SINGAPORE, AND

A BRUSH WITH PIRATES

*C*ANADIAN THANKSGIVING had happened to fall on the day that disappeared when we crossed the International Date Line about a month ago. Now American Thanksgiving was fast approaching, and many people on the ship were dreading the prospect. "I'm sick of these Brits and their anti-American rhetoric," said one of my fellow passengers. "If they pull any of that stuff during Thanksgiving dinner, there'll be hell to pay." The U.S.-based passengers had gone to the purser and cook en masse and forced them to prepare turkey, stuffing, and the other traditional Thanksgiving dishes. Wishing to avoid the kind of cultural violence I saw brewing, I bribed the stewardess to bring me some food on a tray.

We were passing islands everywhere – port, starboard, forward, aft. The Moluccas. Not one sign of human occupation on any of the islands and cays we encountered; I assume this meant that they had no permanent sources of fresh water (otherwise they would have boasted time-share condos by now). At one point we were sailing through a

section of tidal straits that was like being part of some river-
ine operation on the Mekong or perhaps the Irrawaddy.
Here trials began on the newly rebuilt Number One engine,
which seemed to be working fine. We picked up so much
speed, in fact, that we revised our time of arrival in Bandar
by one full day.

At this point, the ship's anti-pirate procedures went into
effect: for we were entering the Java Sea, sailing westward
towards Sumatra, with Java to port and the southern coast
of Borneo far off to starboard somewhere. This was pirate
country. Here, groups of renegade Malaysians, Filipinos, and
ethnic Chinese use small fast craft called cigarette boats to
prey on big, clumsy, heavily laden freighters like ours (we
were at this point carrying cargo equal to 93 per cent of our
capacity by weight).

You might imagine from my earlier comments that all
honest pirates had long ago gone *off* the account and taken
jobs as stevedores. Yet piracy remains a genuine threat in
this end of the world, the last reported incident having
occurred only ten days earlier. The thousands of uninhabited little islands in these parts hide a small population
of violent seafaring young men looking for ways to make
their fortunes in a hurry. The *Pride of Great Yarmouth* had
never been pirated, but one of its sister ships had been hit
a couple of years earlier, passing through the Karimata
Strait, north of where we were, between Sumatra and
Borneo, en route to Singapore. A small party from a speeding boat boarded with a grappling hook before the crew
could stop them, and made off with the contents of the
master's safe. Pirates know that, whereas on a cruise ship
the purser's safe is the prize, on a freighter the safe is in the

master's cabin, which is always located immediately below the bridge. I was refused an exact figure, but a ship like the *Pride of Great Yarmouth* typically carries US$200,000 in cash for wages and emergencies. As a friend of mine pointed out later, these pirates are actually more like seafaring bank robbers.

When we had come aboard in England, we had found copies of the company's *Passenger Safety Manual* on our made-up bunks. This encyclopaedic work runs alphabetically from "Abandon Ship" to "Working Parts of the Vessel." By far the most interesting entry is the one under the heading "Pirates." It's intriguing in its coyness:

> Pirates are still a threat to shipping in certain areas of the world. Our vessels regularly transit waters where the threat exists, and specific and well-practised measures are already drawn up on our vessels to counter such dangers. The master and the chief officer will explain all the precautions that are taken, which have been brought into place after extremely careful evaluation of all facets of the problem. Our measures are taken from the recommendations of a number of international forums. Should you have any fears in this regard, do not hesitate to bring them to the master's attention.

When I was in Nouméa, I read a story in *Les Nouvelles Calédoniennes* about a pirate community at Jolo City, on the island of Jolo, part of the Sulu Archipelago between the Philippines and Borneo. I took a cutting of the piece, which read in part:

> Le sud des Philippines n'a pas le monople de la piraterie moderne. Contrabandiers et flibustiers de tous pails infestent les eaux de la mer Rouge, le golfe de Siam, le détroit

de Malacca et le sud des Caribes, le long des côtes Vénézuéliennes. Au total, plus d'un millier d'actes de piraterie sont recensés chaque année par le Bureau maritime international, un organisme indépendant chargé de lutter contre ce fléau – avec un succès limité, il faut bien l'avouer. Sans parler des violiers de plaisance qui n'arrivent jamais à bon port des boat people massacrés par dizaines de milliers en mer de Chine.

The *Pride of Great Yarmouth* still contained much evidence of its previous life as a Soviet icebreaker serving isolated U.S.S.R. military posts. One deck above me, for example, was a little room stuffed with old Soviet communications equipment. This was in addition to the radio shack, which was still up near the bridge, as in the old days. This other area had been the secret signals room, staffed by a Soviet military specialist; no one else was allowed inside, according to a crew member who once sailed on the vessel under its old flag. The military radio officer, my source told me, was not a KGB agent. There had always been a KGB agent aboard, as a matter of policy, he said, but none of the crew knew which officer secretly held that portfolio. Similarly, just around the corner from my cabin was a room with a particularly strong-looking steel door, with two stout hasps for extra-heavy-duty locks. It was perhaps the only door on the ship that was deliberately unmarked. Now the room was being used as storage space for photocopier paper and other stationery; originally, it contained a rack of Kalashnikov automatic rifles.

Merchant ships today, no matter where they ply their trade, rarely have arms lockers, as was common practice as late as the Second World War. The thicket of paperwork surrounding the subject is now so dense that only German shipping companies are prepared to put up with the nuisance. Even American ships usually have no weapons aboard. If they do, such arms are usually limited to a captain's pistol, locked in the safe, presumably as a silent remonstrance against potential mutineers. Locked up, that would be its only conceivable purpose, as it would clearly be next to worthless against the pirate menace. Sparks told me of a ship he had been on in which the safe contained a dangerously obsolete .32-calibre revolver and only four bullets. Six had been issued originally, when the ship was commissioned; over the years, two had been misplaced or taken as souvenirs. One of the *Pride of Great Yarmouth*'s officers told me he believed that there was a set of hand-cuffs aboard for use in extreme emergencies. "Haven't seen the keys for several years, though. They're kicking about here somewhere, I suppose. They'll surface again one day." It's hardly surprising, then, that there were no firearms aboard the *Pride of Great Yarmouth*, at least officially. Some of the Russian crew have been known, out of earshot of the officers, to allow others to infer that, in certain situations, particular well-hidden personal belongings could always be retrieved.

There was, however, a plan for meeting the pirate menace, just as the safety manual promised; the captain revealed it in a two-page memo posted in the common areas. As pirates in this region operate in darkness, the plan was to deny them cover by keeping the ship well lit. Each evening the bosun and his deck crew were to rig as many lights over the side as the electrician could supply. From dusk until dawn, three-man pirate watches would be maintained. They would consist of a man on the fo'c's'le, another on the poop, and a third patrolling back and forth between, all equipped with electric torches and walkie-talkies, and all in contact with one another as well as with the officer on watch and the cadet on the bridge. The memo stated: "Radar to be watched frequently to locate suspicious craft. Sweep area around ship frequently using searchlight. Use nightsight (not in vicinity of bright lights). Keep a close watch on vessels approaching ship's side. Start fire pump if suspicious craft approaches." In the event of an attack, the document continued, these would be the procedures: "Sound alarm if suspect pirate boarding. Sound whistle and P on bells. Make an announcement on broadcast system in English and Russian. Alter course to try to make boarding more difficult. Make announcement on VHF. Show all possible lights." The idea was to make boarding as risky as we could and then, if a boarding party looked as if it might gain a foothold, to shoot them with the fire hoses, which the deck crew would have already lashed to the bulwarks for immediate use. The captain's order concluded: "All external doors to be secured at night except for bridge wing doors, which will be secured by rope from inside, in order that patrolmen can come in and out. Doors can be opened by day except in Bandar Lampung, where they should be kept locked. Radio officer to have telex prepared with emergency message in case boarded."

Two nights after the memo went up, the third mate, who had the watch from 2000 to 2400 hours, picked up two presumed pirate boats on the radar screen. He was right in the middle of his watch, and we were in the corner of the Java Sea between Java and Sumatra, having left behind the farthest-flung industrial suburb of Jakarta but not yet neared our eventual destination of Bandar Lampung. The first blip was a racing boat, containing, the third mate believed, four people. He clocked it at thirty-five knots, and it circled us twice, counter-clockwise. We were doing seventeen knots. Both passes were right under the rail, within boarding distance. Meanwhile, the second craft, bigger but much slower and holding an undetermined number of people, stayed right on our stern. The third mate assumed that the first was probing our defences or making a feint for the other. He woke the captain (who usually retired at 2000 hours and rose by 0500). They didn't sound the general alarm or the klaxon, or send the distress telex, or even turn on the hoses. Instead, they stirred the crew and kept the big lights shining in the faces of the presumed pirates, who knew that, while they needed to get only a single armed man aboard us to do the job, they must do so with surprise on their side. They sailed off into the darkness, presumably to pick on someone else, on some other night. The captain wrote a full report for London and pledged everyone present to secrecy, lest the affair adversely affect passenger sales. But of course many of us were still awake at that hour, and in any case, no one could keep a secret on a ship of the *Pride of Great Yarmouth*'s size.

Another traditional problem of life at sea still haunts captains and shipowners. To quote again from the *Passenger Safety Manual*: "Stowaways present the Company with considerable difficulty, because of proving nationality and the restrictions and expenses in guarded repatriation of such individuals." A British marine-insurance association estimates that about 15,000 cases are investigated each year, a figure it gladly concedes is conservative. Most stowaways are males less than thirty years of age, and most sneak aboard their unwilling host vessels in Africa, Eastern Europe, or South America (especially Peru), bound, they hope, for ports in the United States, Canada, or France, to rank the top three destinations in order of popularity. "If at any time you suspect that a person has stowed away, please contact the master or a senior officer so that a thorough search of the vessel can be made before it leaves port. The situation is so serious in some parts of the world that it is routine to search a vessel before sailing from port. Your assistance here as another pair of eyes will be greatly appreciated."

When I left Canada (which charges airlines and shipping companies $7,000 for deporting each stowaway), a big ongoing news story concerned four Filipino sailors pleading for refugee status on the grounds that their lives wouldn't be safe if they were sent packing from the country. They were crew aboard a Taiwanese container ship, part of the state-controlled Yang Ming Line. The men had blown the whistle on the alleged murder of several stowaways at sea. After departing, I was, for all intents and purposes, beyond the reach of the media, and did not know the outcome of the hearing. But I knew that the sort of story the sailors told is all too often true. In many parts of the world it is accepted that any stowaways found at sea in international waters will be stripped and thrown overboard.

In many cases, however, the stowaway's death aboard ship actually alerts crew to his presence. Fully containerized ships are the biggest problem. Sometimes corrupt shipping agents will sell a stowaway a place in a container where, as thousands of such containers are packed all together, he will probably go undetected, until he dies of exposure. On break-bulk freighters, stowaways are sometimes hidden in sealed holds, where they are likely to suffocate, especially when the hold, previously used to carry some agricultural commodity, is fumigated before it is sealed tight.

Stowaways did not surface on the *Pride of Great Yarmouth*, which doesn't go to the preferred destinations in North America, though it does call at some desperately poor places in the Pacific, where potential stowaways could try to slip aboard. As for the opposite problem – ship-jumpers – the *Pride of Great Yarmouth*, I was told, does not have much difficulty. "In the past, when a lot of the crew were Bangladeshi, sometimes one would desert with shore leave, or even without," my source informed me. When discovered, this too resulted in big fines being assessed against the owners and the underwriters. It also led to a sentry being posted at the gangplank during all calls in port. "Since we've gone with the trend, you might say, and used predominantly Russian crews, the problem has disappeared completely. The Russians are good hard workers. They're not going anywhere. To them, this is a highly desirable job. You're well fed and looked after, you work outdoors, you go to the South Pacific where it's warm, and you get paid in American dollars, cash. You even get overtime. Believe me, this is Russian Orthodox heaven."

The Russians I talked with were somewhat less sanguine, although they didn't totally contradict the gist of this. In addition, many sailors, regardless of nationality, particularly enjoy tramp freighters because of the possibility of spending an unspecified amount of time in some exotic place they might not have considered visiting or wouldn't have been able to see from a fast-in-and-out container vessel. Which leads me to this last stray fact, for which I am grateful, again, to Christopher Buckley's book *Steaming to Bamboola*. According to Buckley, just as respiratory diseases constitute the principal occupational hazard for tanker crews, so veneral disease is that of tramp freighter crews. He does not elaborate. He doesn't need to.

By the time we neared Singapore, the voyage was getting stranger and stranger. One day, for no apparent reason, the ship was suddenly infested by small pea-green grasshoppers. They penetrated every part of the vessel. Some people even found them lurking in their trouser cuffs. Then, just as quickly, they were gone. Soon after, and more alarmingly, the decks were thick with big shiny black beetles with fierce-looking horns. They were the rhinoceros beetle (*Sewoganathus arfakainias*), which, including horn, are about the same diameter as the depression in a tea saucer and are the bane of copra planters. No doubt ours had come aboard with one or more of the cargoes of copra, perhaps escaping from the hold during the fire. Now they were everywhere, especially the males, which have a big claw to distinguish them. The Wopkai people of PNG, who live near the Irian Jaya border, prize the horns as body orna-ments. After two days, these creatures, too, disappeared as quickly and mysteriously as they had come.

On the way to Bandar Lampung, we passed schools of small fishing boats of local design. They rode very low in the water and had upswept prows and long canopies strung up to keep off the piercing morning sun. We also passed fascinating little islands that looked like an engraved frontis-piece for Robert Louis Stevenson: a saddle formation with enormous limestone caves, with surf lapping inside them. They were uninhabited. Forest fires were visible in the distance. Was it because of the Indonesian forest fires that we were picking up a load of charcoal for feedering to Singapore for trans-shipment? Our main chore at Bandar was loading and unloading containers, which we began to do as soon as we tied up at the Panjamp Container Terminal, using the terminal's huge gantries, a quick if expensive way to get the job done.

Bandar is actually two cities, the port of Telukbetung and its hilltop neighbour Tanjunkarang. Like most such products of amalgamation, it is somewhat formless, without an obvious centre (or a culture?) of its own. Bandar spreads out in three directions from the harbour located at the southern tip of Sumatra, the homes of the well-off sitting side by side with those of the poor, new construction going on everywhere, red ants falling from the trees when the wind blows, which is seldom. The cars were new and the traffic heavy, the wide streets seemed narrow with the clots of vendors on both sides. During the run-up to Christmas, or rather to the Christmas retailing season, Christianity of a sort is almost as much in evidence as Islam. I saw women in chadors and Catholic schoolgirls in their own prescribed uniforms. In the course of one day I heard "All I Want for Christmas Is My Two Front Teeth" played in a shop and the call to prayer ringing through the streets.

The retired doctor turned out to be much motivated by sexual fantasy. When a mob of the schoolgirls passed, he said to me conspiratorially, "Ah, look at all those heavenly young knockers. Don't they take your breath away?" Before I could come up with a suitably neutral response, the doctor, who was always most prosperous-looking with his deep tan, sharply creased white linen trousers, and two Rolex

watches (one set to GMT, the other to local time), was
approached by a male prostitute of about eighteen. A verbal
scuffle followed, with the rent-boy saying, "Do you speak
English? I would prefer it, sir" and the doctor, red-faced,
sputtering, "I *am* speaking English, you worthless infidel."
In the space of two seconds, his self-image as a *Guardian*
reader, a person who prided himself on exuding tolerance
and worshipping diversity, had disappeared. Before an ugly
scene could develop, the doctor's wife returned. She had
been inside one of the batik shops, bargaining.

I browsed there briefly, enough to see how Judeo-Christian
as well as Muslim motifs have influenced local design; a pair
of batik wall-hangings, for example, were clearly intended
to relate the story of Noah and the Ark. I also couldn't avoid
noticing, here and elsewhere during our call at Indonesia,
that certain frocks come with belts from which hang plastic
replicas of gold coins; at a distance I assumed that they
were meant to look like sovereigns. But no. On close inspection I found that they were – of course – copies of the
Dutch guilders of the 1920s. This is a curious relic of Dutch
colonialism, an experience from which modern Indonesia
has learned only how to control others, playing regional
villain in long-drawn-out territorial wars in places as small
as East Timor and as large as Irian Jaya. When we straggled
back to the ship towards evening (the ship was sometimes
our fortress as well as our prison), we heard the muezzin
call the faithful to prayer once more, his voice wavering
from the nearest mosque through the hot, still air.

We returned to find an incipient crisis. The itinerary,
which was continuously in a state of flux, had been revised

to suggest that we would be in Singapore for only a few hours, and then only at night. We were to arrive in three days, at 2200 hours. Singapore would be our last stop for shore food, newspapers, stretching our legs, telephoning home, and performing such necessary tasks as getting eyeglasses, shoes (and our bodies) repaired until we reached Antwerp and began to discharge copra. The crew felt cheated as much as the passengers did. Sensing the mood and weighing his options, calculating the efficiency resulting from each equation, the captain elected to anchor in the roads overnight and take us into Singapore at daybreak, thus giving everyone a full day (albeit a Saturday) in port.

The ship's mission in Singapore was to unload containers, a big load of coffee, and some odds and ends, including what in my youth was called a steamroller (I don't know what they're called now). Of course, I was instantly reminded of the steamroller in the 1935 Clark Gable–Jean Harlow picture *China Seas*, which comes loose during a typhoon, crushing some coolies to death: an accident of great moment to Gable, the captain of a coaster, because the steamroller was where he had hidden the secret shipment of gold bullion, to keep it from falling into the hands of pirates. Those were the days when escapism really fled. We were also heading to Singapore to fill up the oil bunkers, as we wouldn't be refuelling again until Europe. We bade farewell to the popular fourth engineer (his sea-time up to date, he was going back to the classroom) and welcomed his replacement, a Russian from the agency.

❧

I had never seen so much deep-water shipping in one place as when we tied up at the end of Pasin Panjang in the main cargo area of Singapore, which rivals Hong Kong for the title of busiest port in Asia. In fact, comparisons of the two cities are inevitable in any number of areas. As I made my rounds, I couldn't help but return again and again to the construction "Singapore on the one hand, Hong Kong on the other" – and "Kuala Lampur on a third hand" (one mustn't forget Kuala Lampur, even if one must become a tridexter). Politically, Singapore is a city-state. Geographically, it perches at the tip of the rich Malay Peninsula. The decade before Singapore's independence from Britain in 1959 was marked by student riots, labour strife, and the communist insurgency that was endemic to that postwar construct, the Federated States of Malaysia. Once Malaya became Malaysia in 1963, with KL its capital, Singapore broke away, in 1965, rather than remain in the position of only half-independence that would become so common in the Pacific.

The first leader of independent Singapore was Lee Kuan Yew, a social democrat, and his People's Action Party (PAP) has ruled ever since (today holding 81 of the 83 elected seats in parliament, in 47 of which it ran unopposed). But like the Kuomintang in Taiwan, the PAP long ago put its original leftward leanings behind it. Lee was succeeded in 1990 by Goh Chok Tong, who has pushed ahead with Singapore's evolution as an authoritarian paradise where business is king. The populace is kept in check with continuous material prosperity, and the $10 banknote depicts a luxury public-housing project. And Lee Kuan Yew is still very much a presence. The best-known quotation attributed to him claims that "the government will not be blackmailed." William Safire, the former speechwriter for Richard Nixon, who serves as the right-wing pillar of the *New York Times* op-ed page, has called Lee a "tin pot tyrant" and "Dictator Lee" (*Times*, November 14, 1996). I cite the date because libel suits are not only an important weapon in Singapore's politics, used to prevent opposition leaders from rising by crippling them financially, but also a device to ensure that the outside world maintains correct attitudes towards the city-state. As recently as 1995, Lee personally sued the *International Herald Tribune*. At issue were suggestions that Lee was using Singapore's courts to crush dissent. Singapore's courts found the newspaper and the writer guilty. Another tactic is simply to limit the importation of foreign media products. The *Far Eastern Economic Review*, hardly a journal of anti-business agitation, sold 10,000 copies a week in Singapore until 1987, when it published a piece about Singapore that the government found unflattering. The magazine's Singapore bureau was closed down and only 6,000 copies of future issues could be imported (after ten years the figure was raised to 8,000 – a major breakthrough). Singapore is now fighting to control citizen access to the Internet, lest the populace be inundated with "western values" (a loaded phrase) about democracy and human rights. Yet this is no telecommunications backwater that blocks out people's computer screens; Singapore's four million residents enjoy a per capita income on par with that of western Europe. Fully one-third of the population subscribes to telephone paging services. Historically, free seaports have also been free zones of information and ideas. That's what made Venice and Genoa great in the fifteenth century, or London in the nineteenth, or New York in the twentieth. Singapore, it seems, is trying to sever this connection between trade and culture. So far it has succeeded, and without resorting to Malaysia's tactic of constantly monitoring the Net for all mentions of itself, searching for people it can sue.

The case in Singapore that recently caught the attention of North Americans focused on the fate of an American student, Michael Fay, who was sentenced to six strokes of the cane in 1994 for spraying graffiti on a parked car. The spectacle of a U.S. citizen in the prisoner's dock put Singapore's strict penal code in the international spotlight. The lesson is not merely that Singapore canes people for petty vandalism (or fines them as much as S$50 for jaywalking and S$1,000 for littering), but also that it gives ten years in prison to marijuana smokers and hangs those found with five hundred grams of the stuff, that homosexuality is strictly outlawed, and that dissident political views are sometimes silenced under the Official Secrets Act. Yet this is not Bucharest of a generation ago but modern Singapore, city of orchids and frangipani trees, a treat for the eye and the other senses, where violent crime is almost unheard of, unemployment is enviably low (2.7 per cent at the close of 1997), and the races (77 per cent Chinese, 14 per cent Malay, and 7 per cent Indian) live in harmony in a way that would have seemed impossible during the race riots of the 1960s. Mutual prosperity is the key; lines between race are not economic lines as well, as in Fiji, say. Also, Singapore is a secular republic, tolerating all the various religions of its people, in contrast to Malaysia next door, which is officially a (moderate) Islamic state.

Singapore can be used as a revealing test of western liberalism. In Singapore, smoking is allowed only in private homes and cars for the most part. Most of the North Americans I talk with would probably agree with this, finding the strictures tough but necessary for public health. In Singapore, spitting or urinating in elevators is a serious matter; so is throwing garbage from rooftops. Again, who could disagree? But what of some attempts to control viewpoint and purely private behaviour? Don't they strike us as unpleasant reminders of our own political pasts? In Singapore, *Fanny Hill* and Henry Miller are still banned by the chillingly named Ministry of Information and the Arts (whereas in the West they're simply no longer taken seriously). In fact, Singapore still bans books that even the Vatican gave up on long ago. The present list of English-language books and magazines not allowed in Singapore includes such obviously obsolete political tracts as *Malay's Case for Independence*. Chewing or importing gum is illegal. So are chocolates in the shape of gold coins. So are "playing cards bearing nude or bare-bosomed female human figures" and other such sexual kitsch. There is even a rule against "spontaneous acts of kindness," though I couldn't find anyone who could tell me exactly what this means. Singapore's appellate court recently ruled that male-female oral sex is illegal unless followed by genital intercourse. As part of the Smile Singapore campaign designed to encourage tourism, authority figures such as immigration officers are issued small mirrors, in order that they might remind themselves always to grin invitingly. A Canadian judge who recently studied the judiciary in Singapore told the media back home of the "insidious fear that pervades the society" and the "veneer of democracy and free speech in areas like trade and commerce" that hide what he called the people's fear of their government (this reported, a bit surprisingly, in the pro-government *Straits Times*). Myself, I have always believed, along with Thomas Jefferson, that a healthier situation is for the government to be slightly afraid of the people. In any case, so far the new Singapore has held together nicely – that is, profitably – but there is trouble on the horizon.

Like Hong Kong, this small island (42 kilometres [25.2 miles] wide and 25 kilometres [15 miles] high) has no natural resources other than its harbour. To stay competitive with Malaysia, Singapore is adding to its port facilities just as frantically as it is building everything else (construction cranes being an almost permanent feature of the skyline). Meanwhile, Malaysia, with 18 million people, is spending even more to give the edge to Port Kelang, which serves Kuala Lampur. Taking a cue from Hong Kong during its last colonial days, KL is also building a new international airport (on what until recently was a palm-oil plantation). Both projects will weaken Singapore's primacy in fields as different as tourism and finance. Looking ahead a decade or so, many see a diminished rank for Singapore in a redrawn map of the region. There is even speculative talk of Singapore perhaps rejoining Malaysia – speculative and heretical talk, given the bitterness of the split-up.

Still, it was a pleasure to be in Singapore, having a real cup of coffee (there was only instant on the ship) and reading the historic old *Straits Times* (and, after looking over my shoulder, its cheekier rival, *New Paper*) – searching, as I sat and sipped, for some tangible evidence of the *old* Singapore.

You won't find it at the Raffles Hotel and its associated shopping concourses. You won't find it in Chinatown or Little India either, both of which are sanitized miniature reconstructions, aimed at tourists, of the many acres of shophouses and such that have been pulled down for high-rises. Singapore is a theme park of itself. This was hardly the case a generation or more ago.

The Singapore of, let us say, 1935 was a city of approximately one million, of whom two-thirds were Chinese. Its pace of trade was less frantic than that of Hong Kong, but the mixture of races and languages was far richer. Perhaps partly for this reason, and also because it was so much more southerly and tropical than Hong Kong, Singapore seemed more decidedly colonial. Its tone and style were closer to those of, for instance, Rangoon than to those of Shanghai. Singapore's economy was resource-based, but tourism could not be denied its place. "At certain times of the year," wrote Alex Dixon, a retired police officer, in his memoir *Singapore Patrol* (1935), "world-cruising liners visited Singapore, to the enrichment and delight of taxi-drivers, shopkeepers, and snake-charmers." The ships' passengers rushed to the rail and "stared wonderingly at the quivering panorama of the islands, and smiled at the antics of the diving boys alongside." Many of these tourists, Dixon observed, were Americans, "decent folk from the Middle West who had pinched and saved all their lives to pay for one romantic excursion to the unknown. One wished that they could have had better value for their money."

Singapore, then and now, did not believe in advertising its sins too blatantly. But a vast and complex demi-monde certainly existed there. Dixon, who came out from England in 1927, spent five years as a police detective. Two fatal shootings and one fatal stabbing occurred his first day on the job. He left a fascinating account of this milieu, and of the colony itself, in sometimes heat-prostrated colonial prose, of which the following are samples:

> A lorry rumbled past, stacked high with cases of sheet rubber. Behind me a steamer discharged steel girders while half-naked Tamil coolies chanted monotonously under its swinging derricks. Something of the old, unchanging East lingered in the shadowed vault of a godown, where dark figures moved silently between shining pyramids of tin ingots. . . .

> Our car moved slowly through the press of the streets. There were no idlers in the gloomy, low-pitched shops, and many craftsmen plied their trade by the roadside. Black-smiths' shops were as thick as taverns in Bristol. Standing side by side with cavernous stores, where the devout could buy joss-paper and red candles, were the hovels of copper-smiths, carpenters, and coffin-makers. . . .

> Chinese beggars, emaciated and rheumy, cumbered the pathway. Dock coolies gambled and quarrelled in tight groups under the indulgent eye of a Sikh constable. Others stood, sat, or sprawled full-length before the door. The shafts of two rickshaws rested on the steps of the entrance while their pullers slept, open-mouthed, in the blinding sunlight. Flies settled on their lounging bodies, and, if stirred, spread in a dark buzzing cloud to the offal of the gutter. . . .

> I remember a street which at first sight appeared to be uninhabited; but keener scrutiny revealed that the doors of its closely shuttered houses were conveniently ajar. At one corner of the street the yellow beam of a lantern shows a Sikh watchman dozing, staff in hand, before an elaborate

gateway. The pungent smell of opium caught my nostrils –
raw Persian stuff, which the seasoned smoker prefers to the
adulterated compound sold in Government *chandu* shops.

Opium dens were indeed one of the abiding concerns of the
frankly corrupt colonial police force, whose detective bureau
was run by Europeans and employed Chinese, Indians,
Malays, Bugis, Javanese, Boyanese, Arabs (and one Japanese).
In 1936, taxes on opium still accounted for an astonishing
25 per cent of the budget of the Straits Settlements, the
administrative umbrella that included four main British
outposts – Singapore, Penang, Malacca, and Labuan – and
assorted minor ones. Prostitution was also rampant, to a
degree almost unimaginable in the strait-laced independent
city-state of today. The nature of the subject, however,
means that writers have tended to view it nostalgically:
prostitution, like fresh fruit, it seems, always tasted better
in the old days, whenever the old days happened to be.

The British journalist and diplomat Bruce Lockhart went
back in 1935 to the Malay Peninsula where he had worked
as a rubber planter at about the time of the Great War. In
the resultant book, *Return to Malaya*, his observations are
tough-minded at first:

> Singapore deserved a certain reputation for vice. The vice
> itself was never at any time so lurid or so glamorous as it is
> still painted by certain travellers and by the scenario writers
> of Hollywood. The reputation may die slowly, but now it
> is certainly not deserved. Here, too, change has worked a
> minor miracle.

Then he gives in to sexual melancholy:

> Singapore was the first city in which I had ever seen at first-
> hand the sale and purchase of vice, and the temptation to

revisit what had then seemed the street of adventure was irresistible. Accordingly, just after sunset on the evening of my third day I ordered my chauffeur to drive me to Malay Street and Malabar Street, where formerly the white wrecks of European womanhood and young Japanese girls, silent, immobile and passionless, traded their bodies for the silver dollars of Malaya. As I drove down the beach front, the lights began to appear on the ships in the harbour like so many little lives which would vanish in the morning, for Death is still an early caller in these tropical parts. There was the faintest of cooling airs from the sea. By the time I reached Malay Street it was already dark.

I had chosen this hour intentionally for my attempted recapture of the spirit of a past which had eluded me ever since my arrival. Recognition returned with a momentary thrill, as I made my way into the district inhabited by the poorest Chinese. Somewhere in these narrow streets were houses where secret societies still held their meetings and where another set of laws and moral codes held sway. . . . Malay Street itself brought me face to face with the new Singapore. Gone was Madame Blanche with her . . . frail army of white women recruited by the professional pimps from the poorest population of Central and Eastern Europe, and drifting farther East as their charms declined, *via* Bucharest, Athens and Cairo, until they reached the *ultima Thule* of their profession in Singapore.

There had been no English girls among them. On political grounds the British administration has always maintained a ban on the British prostitute. But here in the past, ships' officers of every nationality, and globe-trotters, travellers, miners and planters from up-country wasted their money on an orgy to which drink and noise and occasional brawling supplied a discordant orchestra. Sometimes, a Malay princeling or Chinese towkay [householder] would make his way discreetly to this sordid temple in order to satisfy an exotic and perhaps politically perverted desire for the embraces of a forbidden white woman.

Gone, too, were the long rows of Japanese brothels with
their lower windows shuttered with bamboo poles behind
which sat the waiting odalisques, discreetly invisible,
magnificent in elaborate head-dress and brightly coloured
kimonos, heavily painted and powdered, essentially
doll-like and yet not without a certain charm which in
Romantic youths like myself inspired a feeling more of
pity than desire....

Two responses are obvious. The first is that, for a younger
generation, 1935 was in fact the dawn of vice in Singapore,
not its dusk; what Lockhart was saying was that Malay Street
had faded as a place of business for White Russian, French,
Greek, and Hungarian prostitutes, while their places had
been taken, in other districts, by Asian women, who quickly
dominated the ship-borne trade. Unlike the Europeans,
many of whom were self-employed, the Asian women were
in the clutches of well-organized rings. This leads to the
second observation: that people like Lockhart could per-
ceive such changes in racial terms alone; that even in what
he undoubtedly believed were the innocent musings of an
old hand, he still manages to expound the racism that is at
the heart of the Anglo-European experience in Asia.

In the 1920s, Singapore became the first large-scale permanent British military base in the Far East. British culture
followed the flag. By 1934, the Singapore Racecourse was
called, no doubt correctly, the finest in the world, with cane
bottoms on all the seats and lifts in the grandstands. As in all
the major East Asian ports, the transplanted British (and,
later, American) way of life flourished alongside a helter-
skelter collision of other civilizations. As Malay Street was
to vice, so Change Alley was to commerce. Indians, Chinese,

Japanese, Arabs, and Jews bartered for everything from socks to fountain pens to European films, while cramped upper-floor offices along either side held lawyers' lairs, gents' hairdressers, and the aromatic offices of dealers in pepper or tapioca. Unregistered brokers flourished unmolested.

Police work extended of course to the more familiar European district, called Tanglin. Officers such as Dixon were not much concerned with commercial practice, but they were obsessed with what they saw as the biggest threat to its continued existence: political subversion. Agents of the Kuomintang, the Chinese nationalist party that for a while was still almost as much communist as fascist in the transitional period following the death of Sun Yat-sen, had agents throughout Singapore. The police kept track of them.

As for crime in the dominant Chinese section of the city, whose most notorious thoroughfare was Sago Street, Dixon was informed on his arrival that it was "terrorized by Cantonese gunmen [called 'five-finger generals' who] belong to the secret societies, which organize street-fighting and armed gang-robberies [and who] shoot informers and detectives on sight." In time, Dixon became an authority on tongs and triads, including the location of their *pangkengs* (lodges) and the signs and signals by which members recognized one another.

> Even the routine work of the Bureau was varied and inter-
> esting, and took us by night and by day into the more
> exciting and disreputable corners of the city. Native and
> European hotels, lodging-houses, and pawnshops were
> regularly visited. Brothels, opium dens, and gambling
> "schools" had to be closely watched, and were occasionally

raided. We were always on the look-out for arms and drug smugglers, and our detectives mixed freely with boatmen, tally-clerks, and dock-coolies in search of information about drug-runners. From time to time our attention was claimed – to a greater or less degree – by pirates, counterfeiters, prostitutes, and confidence tricksters.

Only after much searching did I find one block of what I could see was the original goods. Virtually within the shadow of the new seventy-five-storey Stanford Hotel (the world's tallest, of course) stands a row of rundown traditional Chinese buildings, with their upswept gable-ends – designed to ward off demon spirits – rotting gently away.

The one on the corner was a particularly fascinating structure. Old men in brightly patterned shirts, and with flip-flops on their feet, lounged on the front stoop. (In another city, they would be smoking cigarettes.) The sign above the door, in English and in the old-style Chinese characters, read "Singapore Lorry-Owner's Association." The atmosphere outside was exactly that of a neighbourhood Democratic Party office I once stumbled upon in a desolate section of Chicago. This was clearly a benevolent association, a perpetual-motion political machine, an informal tong, and those old men were fixers. I was relieved to see that Singapore has not quite eradicated every honest trace of the past, and I smiled at the fact that the fixers were the ones to be spared.

I spent my last hours in the new Singapore in a Seattle-style coffee bar. This is the latest fad in the area, where the name Seattle suggests only one thing – software fortunes. All the dishes on the menu had Pacific Northwest references in their names, and there were large photo-murals of Seattle along one wall. What struck me most strongly, however, were the tablecloths. They were paper, and in the centre of each was a jar of felt-tipped pens and a pocket calculator (chained down, like a post-office ballpoint); customers are encouraged to work out the math on whatever deal they're discussing. I had sidled up to a freshly vacated table before the waiter could change the paper, and I sat down to a dazzling mess of doodling, involving, along with Chinese characters, a lot of complicated mathematical symbols, the sort I'm surprised to see anyone still knows (because I, frankly, do not). The server arrived and started to tear away the sheet, but I asked her if I could keep it. She thought I was crazy, but didn't seem able to remember any law I would be violating. I folded the sheet several times and stuffed it into my pocket. This was a true souvenir of Singapore.

10

THE LONG WAY

BACK HOME

$\mathcal{A}$s WE DEPARTED Singapore, I calculated that England was a bit more than 8,000 nautical miles away, via the Suez Canal. Crossing the Indian Ocean, we didn't lay eyes on India itself, but we did pass within 13 kilometres (8 miles) of Sri Lanka, close enough to be winked at by its alabaster lighthouses. By the time we entered the Arabian Sea, on the eighty-eighth day of the voyage, the rebuilt Number One engine was performing so well, and burning so cleanly, that it put Number Two to shame – until, of course, it broke down yet again (but then only briefly).

As we passed close to the Maldives, headed for the entrance to the Red Sea, the sky took on the complexion of molten lead, and then it began to rain. This weather kept up for days, and had a depressing effect on everyone aboard. The worst affected was likely Seagrams, who embarked on a series of mini-benders and resumed insulting everyone, until she was finally reproached. Then, as if suddenly hyper-conscious of "manners," she began pausing every time she entered the dining room to take a whiff of each armpit, to make sure she was not perspiring. In fact, the stench of liquor emanating from her masked any other odour. A dark cloud seemed to form over the table whenever she took her seat. I would not have been surprised to learn that she was the only person ever to flunk the free personality test at the Church of Scientology.

At about this point we experienced a twisted moment of reality when, during our regular weekly fire drill, a real fire broke out and had to be vanquished. During lunch, a couple of hours later, Sasha the cook, having received a rocket from the purser, had the stewardesses lined up and was berating them very loudly and at length. Apparently one of them – the one who seemed to believe she was Marilyn Monroe reincarnate, and whose delivery had become more and more breathless as the months went by – had been smoking a cigarette in the galley, and had inadvertently caused the blaze.

The next day we entered the Gulf of Aden and could see the headlands of Somalia. Poor Somalia. First the war, then the famine, and now devastating floods. All the while, the warlords were in Egypt, yet again dividing up the spoils. One more day and we were in the Red Sea off Yemen, amid numerous small tankers, which seemed to huddle together for protection, since the weather was still foul. Indeed, the Red Sea looked as though it could do with another parting. I fell into conversation with the purser, who told me that we should have exactly enough provisions to get back to Europe, with not a day's more. Since leaving Britain, he informed me, we'd gone through almost two tonnes of potatoes and the same amount of meat. "Eight hundred kilos beef, 800 kilos chicken, 400 kilos other and assorted, including mutton and pork." He also took me down below to show me the sick bay. This was not a surgery but rather a complete hospital room, to be used in case anyone had to be isolated from the rest of the ship's company. Next to it was a room of medical stores, including, I noticed, three zippered body bags of heavy black PVC. "Unfortunately," said the purser, "when this vessel had the only casualties I'm aware of, in October 1995, we had three bodies and only two bags. A seaman died in an empty tank from toxic fumes, and so did his two mates who tried to rescue him."

When we exited the Red Sea and entered the Gulf of Suez, oil rigs were the first things we saw, all of them on the Saudi side, none at first on the Egyptian. There was still more tanker traffic and also, I was delighted to see, one Arab dhow (though motorized). The weather turned cold. Pullovers were brought out of chests and closets. Suez was even windier than New Zealand. We had probably seen the last of the good weather.

The day before we entered the Suez Canal, the myth of our ability to repel pirates was shattered. Two parties of "boatmen" (Egyptian junk dealers) threw ladders over the side and clambered aboard with no resistance. They carried with them all their goods, such as fake Rolex watches, leather-veneer jackets, beaten-brass plates, dollar postcards, and cottons that seemed to shrink as you touched them. All of the vendors were related, by blood or marriage, to Suez pilots. Having them aboard, permitting them to sleep on the deck overnight, and allowing them to set up shop outside the dining salon was part of the price of getting through the canal. We were even forced to use our cranes to pick up the two small boats they travelled in. Such throwbacks to the days of the caravans were, like the cash and endless cartons of Marlboro cigarettes, necessary to ensure a safe, prompt passage through Suez. For some reason, the vendors attempted to mimic the nationality of whomever they were selling to. One of them wore a kilt and called himself Jock. We entered the canal at five-thirty the following morning, second in a long convoy, immediately behind a Panamanian panamax. The transit took all day. Comparisons with the Panama Canal, of course, are unavoidable.

Like the idea of cutting through the Central American isthmus, the idea of slicing through the isthmus of Suez, joining Africa and Asia, was already old before any practical steps were taken. In fact, an east-west canal, linking the Nile with the Red Sea, as distinct from a north-south one joining the Red Sea to the Mediterranean, actually operated in ancient times, but was filled in by a local ruler during the eighth century CE to hinder enemy invasion. Napoleon, among others, saw of what great value a Suez canal up the Sinai would be, but, as we know, it was left to Lesseps, the French engineer and promoter, to obtain a ninety-nine-year lease from the khedive of Egypt, Said Pasha, and get down to the business of building one. He began construction in 1859 and finished a decade later, fully 100 per cent over budget. Part of the deal was that the facility would be open to shipping of all nationalities, and they would all benefit from its obvious convenience; a transit of the canal would cut the length of a voyage from London to Bombay, for example, almost in half.

Matters began to go awry in 1875. Said Pasha's successor, Ismail Pasha, became financially embarrassed and sold off his interest to the British. Mind you, the British did, in

1885, guarantee the right of other countries to use the canal, under the terms of what was to be called the Convention of Constantinople (1888), and also the right to its own continued use once Egypt became independent. This independence came to pass in 1936. But twelve years later, when Israel was created, Egypt refused to let Israeli shipping use the canal, or even, with brief respites now and then, to let non-Israeli ships through carrying Israeli cargo. The situation was resolved by stages, one point at a time, following a series of international crises. In 1956, with a dozen years left to run on the lease, the Egyptian president, Gamal Abdel Nasser, nationalized the canal. This precipitated the Suez Crisis, in which Israeli forces occupied the Sinai, and Britain and France (and, later, UN troops) took up positions along the canal. Damage from the 1956 fighting is still visible, though you need an expert eye to distinguish it from that done during the Six-Day War of 1967, which signalled an eight-year shutdown. From 1957 until the Egyptian–Israeli peace accord of 1979, no Israeli ships passed through these waters. This coincided with a period of sharp commercial decline for the canal.

As late as the early 1960s, the Suez Canal handled 15 per cent of all international shipping, and petroleum from the Persian Gulf made up three-quarters of the tonnage. By 1980, only 4 per cent of all shipping moved through the canal, and only a third of it was petroleum products. What happened? Years of instability, coupled with years of what shipowners saw as Egyptian price-gouging. The *Pride of Great Yarmouth*, for example, spent £45,000 to use the Panama Canal. Admittedly we were much lighter at that time; and, in fact, we were returning to Europe now with only eight tonnes of unused cargo capacity. Still, our charge for using the Suez Canal was a comparatively outrageous £70,000. Lately, the Egyptians have been offering bargain discounts, but they can do nothing about some of the other causes of the canal's steep decline. One of these is the opening of the Suez–Mediterranean pipeline, whose revenues Egypt must share with the other oil-producing Arab states that helped to build it. Since 1980 there have also been tunnels (now seven in all) dug under the canal. Still another factor is one that Suez has in common with Panama: ships have become bigger and bigger, tankers particularly, while the canal can be enlarged only so much. At present, Suez can accommodate ships drawing up to 18 metres (58.5 feet). Still and all, the Suez Canal handles more than 17,000 vessels a year, roughly the same number that the Panama Canal does.

We began in the Gulf of Suez, passed the city of Suez, then entered the Great Bitter Lake and the Little Bitter Lake, which were long ago joined as one. All the way, throughout the day, the contrast was stark between the west bank, which the Egyptians are developing with resorts and whole new communities, and the east, or Sinai, bank, which is kept relatively empty as a buffer against Israel. Irrigation makes the western side bloom, and investment makes it flower. But the east side is made up of long stretches of dunes, interrupted here and there by a battery park or some other military fixture – or by the rubble of war, which is slow to rust in the dry desert air.

Beyond the Bitter Lakes are Lake Timsah and the city of Ismailia, the headquarters of the canal administration and a place exactly midway through the transit, which, including approaches, is 169 kilometres (105 miles). After Ismailia, the remainder of the canal, nearly a straight line, goes through some even-more-spectacular desert country to the marshes running into Lake Manzala, until, finally, there before us was Port Said, gleaming white city of minarets and construction cranes. At that stage, with evident relief and glee, the captain booted off all the vendors and lowered their boats. They gathered their inventory and scrambled over the side as they had come, speeding off in the opposite direction to await their next prey. The trip took us about the same length of time that the Panama Canal transit had: fifteen hours. A few minutes more and we would be in the Med. Home and England, I knew, wouldn't be far off now. There is an old saying among British sailors coming out of the top of Suez: "Six days to the Rock, five more to the dock." Would we reach Gibraltar within the proverbial six days? Frankly, the weather looked a bit worrisome.

The voyage suddenly took on a new complexion as we sailed westward across the Mediterranean and into the Atlantic. We were closing the circle, heading back to our point of departure. Seagrams hadn't been seen at meals for three days, and Jane once again got the purser to open her cabin with his passkey. They found the floor littered with empty vodka bottles, evidence of a secret stash, and Seagrams in her bunk, sleeping it off. This confirmed our suspicions and put our fears to rest. For more than forty-eight hours, all her fellow passengers had been worried about her. In fact, the collective anxiety brought us together as a group at last, transcending differences of class, accent, and passport.

Jane learned what had pushed Seagrams to the brink. Seagrams, apparently, had travelled on one of the company's ships a year earlier, and had an affair with one of the Russian sailors. They had corresponded, and she had learned that he was now aboard the *Pride of Great Yarmouth*. To surprise him, she had scraped up the money for a second round-the-world passage. However, her turning up unannounced only frightened him. He told her their relationship was over, and retreated to the engine room. She retreated to her liquor cabinet. From this point on, some of the other Russians also became cool to the passengers in general. This too only brought us closer. As Mrs. Murphy said, quoting the Bible as she liked to do, "When struck on the cheek, put your best foot forward."

Like all melodrama, this one played dangerously with both tragedy and comedy. The day following her revelation to Jane, Seagrams again disappeared from view – and from her cabin as well. The officer on watch spotted her from the bridge and sent a squad to fetch her. She was wandering moodily near the bow, staring into the cold water and letting herself be drenched by the spindrift. He feared she might go over the side, voluntarily or otherwise, for we had been warned to expect the worst weather of the trip to date – a superfluous warning, given the look of the cumulo-nimbus clouds and the alarming wind. When she was safely back in her cabin, the doctor kindly interrupted his holiday to give her an injection of some strong sedative.

On our one-hundred-and-second day at sea, there were tremendous lightning storms all day, sudden violent rend-ings, powerful and silent, as we passed the lights of Ceuta to port and those of Gibraltar to starboard. The strait is so narrow – only 13 kilometres (8 miles) – that it looked as though the end of the thread might miss the eye of the needle. We were no sooner through than the really rough weather descended, just as forecast.

I was up most of the night, dealing with shattered glass and flying furniture. The ship pitched so much that I imagined the rudder would never be in the water again, or the bow out of it. There was simultaneous rolling. What was really frightening, though, was the irregularity and unpredictability of the motions, the lack of any assured rhythm. At times you couldn't help but take such weather personally and conclude that the sea was out to destroy your ship in particular. The attitude was all the more easily maintained because one couldn't see outside, so heavily did the rains beat against the (now leaking) glass. I was alone in the dining room at 1800 hours when a rogue wave struck us broadside and overturned one of the heavy tables, propelling it into the captain's table, with great loss of stemware, china, and HP Sauce. The third table, where I sat, crashed into the galley. I had just enough time to lift my plate out of danger when the avalanche began.

Such chaos was wholesale throughout the ship. One of the computers on the bridge came loose from its brackets and landed on the deck – on its back, like a turtle. Fortunately, there was only one injury. Mrs. Murphy was struck on the left knee by a piece of furniture that hurtled through mid-air. She seemed to be hurt seriously, though we didn't believe that the joint was fractured. The next day the weather was a little better (only a little), though the level of confusion rose. The ship's owners, it seemed, had not yet decided which European ports we would be calling at, or in what sequence. Here we were, crossing the almost-always-unpleasant Bay of Biscay, only one day from the

English Channel, two at most, and we were still uncertain of our destination.

When we had booked passage, we had been given to understand that we would be touching at some or all of the following places: Tilbury in Essex, Hull in Yorkshire (now there's a major Europort), Hamburg in Germany, Rotterdam in the Netherlands, Antwerp in Belgium, and Le Havre in France. Our tickets said that we must disembark at the "first U.K. port." But which one would it be, and when? We awaited instructions from London. Meanwhile, I sensed that the weather might have let up a bit more. Either that, or we were becoming used to it. Or maybe all the breakable objects on board had already been smashed.

In three days' time it would be Christmas. This would mean double wages for the crew. It also meant that no stevedores would be working, although all the ports would be open for comings and goings. Most of our copra, the majority of our cargo by volume and weight, was consigned to either Le Havre or Antwerp. So it made sense to visit these places first. All the more so because the stevedores on the European mainland work on Boxing Day, unlike those in Britain. At the same time, the ship was due for its routine maintenance. Certain repairs needed to be done as well, particularly to the communications and navigational equipment, and the contract for such work rests with the U.K. company that supplied it. While awaiting his orders, the captain became unnaturally relaxed and talkative. "My father was at sea fifty years ago, on the Blue Funnel ships on the Britain-to-South-Africa run," he told me. "He was just a junior officer at the time. He had a pet monkey. One voyage, the weather was so bad, off the coast of Portugal, that the monkey actually died of seasickness."

"How many species of primate do you suppose are susceptible?" I asked.

But then a telex began to rattle in, and he chased me off the bridge. The message, I later learned, was a strange compromise. We were to go to Antwerp first, there to unload much of the copra, do the most urgent repairs, discharge most of the crew and await the replacements, and linger inactive through the Christmas holiday, while also taking on stores and fuel. Any passengers who wished would be able to disembark at this point, and the company would arrange air or ferry transport for them to British soil. Following Antwerp, the *Pride of Great Yarmouth* was to sail, not to Tilbury or Hull, but to Felixstowe, the mammoth container port on the Suffolk coast, more or less immediately across the Channel from Antwerp, there to have its annual physical examination and check-up.

As we moved up the Channel, the sea improved enough to permit walks on deck, if you held on, for the winds remained strong. Each of the steel containers stacked amidships had two slots at the bottom to receive the tines of a fork-lift; the sound of the wind entered on one side like a siren and came out the other more like a scream. At least I no longer feared that the bolts holding them in place would sheer off, sending containers into the sea (and, most likely, putting the ship out of balance). Such does happen occasionally. Last trip, the *Pride of Great Yarmouth* lost nine containers in the Bay of Biscay. Such incidents do nothing to lower a ship's insurance premiums or attract repeat customers. Some salvagers, in very weathery places such as

the Canary Islands, pay their overheads by capturing lost
containers and claiming them before they settle to the
bottom. Partly submerged containers are also the primary
manmade dread of the transoceanic yachties who call themselves passage-makers.

So it was, then, that on December 23, day 106 at sea,
we picked up our pilot and began the eight-hour run up
the River Schelde to Antwerp, a port second only to its
rival Rotterdam in Continental Europe. The river was
choked in fog.

I'd never been to Antwerp (the name is probably from
aande-werfen – "on the wharves") and I found Belgium's
second city a place with much of interest. Being Flemish,
not French, it has relatively little in common with Brussels,
but a great deal with Amsterdam. Some of the similarities
are ones of relative size: Antwerp's diamond district is far
larger than Amsterdam's, while its red–light district is much
less vast. Other differences are political. Antwerp's local
government is dominated by the Vlaams Blok, a party often
described as neo–fascist. In addition, the cultural atmosphere is more illiberal than that of Amsterdam – but only
by this comparison. Unlike Singapore, Antwerp is a place
where the arts and personal freedom flourish and where you
could live out your time quite pleasantly without being
particularly aware of the shifts in local politics.

Among the advantages of sea travel is the fact that one
approaches cities as they were first approached, by water,
getting a view that has been so long neglected that it once
again seems fresh. Like so many other places in the world,
Antwerp has abandoned its original port area to tourism
and chance and has built a container terminal and other

such facilities away from the central commercial district. Zandvliet, as it is named, has 96 kilometres (60 miles) of quays and handles 16,000 ships a year. Chugging upriver, you can see at once why Antwerp (Antwerpen in Dutch; Anvers in French) took shape where it did. It is located where the Schelde deteriorates into the Schelde Estuary (whose tides are so high that as recently as a few years ago a French warship, mistiming its departure, found itself immobilized in the muck). The Romans had a large port in Antwerp by the second century BCE, but in ensuing ages, once the Roman empire collapsed and resolved itself into nation- and city-states, Antwerp was left in a quandary. The Schelde marked the boundary between the French- and German-speaking parts of the newly redrawn map. It became an entrepôt, yes, but also a kind of no-man's land.

When you creep up on Antwerp by water and see it as it was meant to be seen, the most prominent landmark is the spire of OLV, *Onae-Lieve-Vrouwekatherdraal* – Our Lady's Cathedral. This boastfully Gothic structure, begun in the fourteenth century, is extremely rich in art (including work by Rubens, the citizen of whom Antwerp is most proud), despite its distinction of having been sacked by both the Protestant Dutch and the Catholic Spaniards (to say nothing of damage done by the Nazis in more recent times). Travelling by river, you also see long rows of empty nineteenth-century wharves, with ornate metal-work on the warehouses. It becomes a simple matter to summon up a sense of what it must have been like when this area was a forest of masts and spars. The warehouses are easy to date, because the Dutch, who still control the maritime approaches, simply closed the port from 1648 to 1863.

The old wharves terminate at the city's other great landmark, the castle called the Steen, as old as the Tower of
London and on a site first fortified by the Vikings.

   With Antwerp, as with most old cities, you can chart the
alternating periods of expansion and contraction by looking
at the changes in architectural fashion. Antwerp's great
period was the transition from the Middle Ages to the
Renaissance when it was one of the most important centres
of learning as well as of commerce. The two went hand in
glove. Even today, after so many wars and other periods of
destruction, the central city looks very old indeed, full
of sixteenth-century buildings of all types and so many
from the seventeenth century that one can be squandered
to accommodate a Pizza Hut (a minor neighbourhood
attraction, like the Frank Sinatra Museum). In an attempt
to recreate the glory days, the Belgians continued to put up
dwellings in the classic Flemish style – narrow frontages,
pitched gables, stepped façades – right into modern times.
The visitor, however, soon learns to date buildings to the
appropriate century according to the texture and colour of
the materials used. Many other landmarks, such as the
Centraalstation, where the railway lines meet, date from
the period of the 1890s and the First World War: the second
great boom, four centuries after the first (and one more of
trade than of civilization in the narrow sense perhaps).
Relics of the two periods make a surprisingly pleasant contrast – and a constant one. Then, in a class by itself, is the
Late Deco office tower now called the Kredietbank Toren.
When it opened in 1930, it was Europe's first skyscraper.
Happily, it was also Antwerp's last.

The *Pride of Great Yarmouth* was docked in Antwerp for six days. On the first, the Murphys departed. Mrs. Murphy needed an X-ray taken of her injured knee before flying back to the United States. She was talking loudly about suing the shipping line for negligence, even though her accident fell clearly into the act-of-God category and we had all signed liability waivers before boarding. She was one of those people for whom litigation is an obsessive pastime, like playing the lotteries, even though she often spoke of such matters with a forced tone of equanimity.

"This trip has been an experience," she said on departure. I expressed agreement.

"It certainly has had its ups and downs," she continued. "But like I always say, let sleeping snakes lie."

"My attitude exactly," I replied. "Let pythons be pythons." She looked puzzled.

New Age was gone, presumably on her way back to Denver. Tim Beneke departed as well, to spend Christmas at home with his family in the States, if he could get a flight from Brussels at that time of year. All the British passengers left, too, taking up the company's offer of free transport to British soil. That left Seagrams and me, and Seagrams felt somewhat indisposed again (and not much fun to be near when she wasn't). I resolved to see the voyage through. Having boarded in Britain, I would not consider the circumnavigation complete until I had returned there by sea and gone ashore.

By this time, many of the Russians were paying out, and the end-of-voyage poker game had begun in the Dirty Mess. Even more Russians, newly recruited, were signing on, so that all the vacated cabins filled up again quickly. On the day before Christmas, I was going down the gangplank for the half-hour journey into central Antwerp when I saw the provisioner's lorry, with some of the sorely needed ship's stores, park astride the dockside rails on which the giant gantries travel as they load and unload containers. I saw what was about to happen yet could do nothing to prevent it: the crane was set in motion, and it struck the food truck amidships, crumpling it like an empty milk carton and scattering our precious vegetables over a wide area. Fortunately no one was injured, but tempers flared.

No dockers were working on Christmas, of course, and again I went into town, where I managed to find a restaurant serving the traditional Christmas dinner (whose tradition?) of turkey curry with boiled rice. When I returned in the late evening, Seagrams had left the ship; I became the last passenger. The unloading of the copra began on Boxing Day and was quite well organized, though the process seemed to me, in my lonely and anxious state, to take an unnaturally long time, regardless. Despite Antwerp's technology, the cargo took as long to discharge here as it did to load in places like Vanuatu and Papua New Guinea.

∾

We set out into the Schelde again on the evening of the twenty-ninth. Despite our considerably lighter load we were travelling very slowly (and not just in comparison to everyone else – though I saw the cross-channel hovercraft moving across the radarscope at thirty-four knots). What should have taken a day or less took us two days, owing to horrible weather (storms in England were causing fatalities), the change of crew, the availability of berthing, and other factors: a frustrating end to the whole enterprise. On New Year's Eve, we arrived at Felixstowe.

I had left Canada in late August and boarded the *Pride of Great Yarmouth* in early September, and had been on the ship for 114 days. In that time, we had crossed 3 oceans and 12 seas, skipped over the Equator twice, made use of the Panama and Suez canals, and called at ports in 9 island nations in addition to the European and Asian mainlands. We had covered almost 30,000 nautical miles. On the outward voyage, I'm told, our ship lost money, but we were so full on the return one that we went into the black.

The next day would be the start of a new year. It would also be my birthday: I was turning forty-nine. I expected to spend the day wandering through the endless containerized wilderness of Felixstowe, looking for a pub that was open. Then I'd figure out how to get home. When I finally arrived back in Toronto, after being stuck one entire night at Heathrow, I found that my wife had moved her possessions out of our house. Later she phoned from an undisclosed location to say that she was filing for divorce, a decision she had made months earlier, on Canadian Thanksgiving (the day I lost entirely when crossing the Date Line). "I've got my lawyer," she said. "You better find yours." In the emotional and legal chaos of the next few months, the voyage of the *Pride of Great Yarmouth* was in danger of being erased from my mind. I have written these pages partly to prove to myself that the trip actually took place.

11

SOUTH PACIFIC SUNSET

*O*UR ROUTE may have taken us round the world but the South Pacific was our destination, our centre of gravity, our reason for being. No other region on Earth carries more romance in its name, but few others must bear up under the unrelieved weight of so many problems at once: racial division, poverty, disease, pollution, the psychological legacy of colonialism, lack of investment, and low productivity. In most other places, such difficulties seem to rank themselves, automatically, into agendas of ever-changing urgency. In the nations of the old Southern Ocean, they all seem equally pressing – and equally insoluble. This too may help account for the region's pull on people's imagination. Once you have been there, even if just passing through, slowly, as we had done, you seem to open a permanent SoPac file in the part of the brain reserved for memories of distant friends you care about. As the Canadian winter made the agonizing transition to Canadian spring, several bits of news, all of them illustrative of this point, seemed to prick my recollection further.

"When in the Kingdom of Tonga," runs the advertise-
ment often found in the *Pacific Monthly* and other regional
media, "stay at the International Dateline Hotel." As though
people just happen one day to find themselves in Tonga
unexpectedly, forced down there during some improbable
jaunt between Fiji and Western Samoa. Yet the ad is crucially
symbolic of several important political currents. The International Dateline Hotel, a smallish affair, is far and away the
biggest such enterprise in the whole collection of far-flung
islands that make up the Tongan nation. Tonga is to the
Pacific as Liberia is to Africa: the only country that was never
colonized by one of the European powers. Its foreign policy
may have been "administered" by Britain from 1900 to
1970, but it was never quite reduced to the status of a vassal
state. Instead, it was, and remains, a monarchy. The International Dateline Hotel was opened in 1967 to commem-
orate the coronation of the present ruler, King Taufa'ahau
Tupou IV, a physically massive man who has turned to
entrepreneurship in an attempt to answer the big question
that surrounds the future of such places in the South Pacific.
The question is this: How can the growing population (in
Tonga's case, over 100,000 people, or more than twice as
many as when His Majesty ascended the throne) support
itself in agricultural conditions best suited to copra and
bananas for the few? Tourism is the obvious alternative. But
the South Pacific already has so many tourists that the
natural beauty the holiday-makers come to see is threatened. The type of callow development that has blighted
Hawaii and Tahiti can only spread.

In 1996, the most recent year for which I can locate
figures, 868,000 tourists visited New Caledonia, PNG, the

Solomons, Vanutatu, Kiribati, the Cook Islands, Niue, French Polynesia, Samoa, and Tonga, all places with delicate ecosystems and delicate economies. At current growth rates, the number will be three million by 2020, or about one-fifth of the long-distance tourist market. At present, Australia, New Zealand, and North America are the main sources of South Pacific tourism, but East Asia and Europe are expected to eclipse them. To accommodate this future, the small South Pacific nations must upgrade their facilities. As I write these words, Pitcairn, population about ninety, the last British colony in the Pacific, has announced that it is giving in to the pressures of modernity and building its first airport – thus destroying the solitude that brought the *Bounty* mutineers in the first place, not to mention the relative handful of visitors subsequently. More tourists in the South Pacific means less truly indigenous culture for them to see and more carefully staged cultural reenactments. How many of the eighty-seven languages spoken in the Solomons will survive the cultural homogenization that follows mass tourism? Linguists report that the number of languages worldwide will be reduced by half during the twenty-first century; they add that, of the six thousand languages now spoken somewhere, at least one hundred have only one native speaker remaining. More visitors mean a dirtier environment as well. One lesson my voyage on the *Pride of Great Yarmouth* taught me is that there is nowhere one can go, on the seas as on land, that humankind has not polluted. What the islanders never saw in their cargo cults was the devastation, the actual threat of extinction, that could accompany too much cargo. I get only a chill when I learn that burials at sea are virtually unheard-of now, not

SO WHAT?

only because of improved shipboard refrigeration, but also because slipping human remains over the side is considered an act of two-way contamination.

Which brings us back to the Kingdom of Tonga and King Tupou IV, who has laboured mightily to bring his people cold cash without harmful consequences. George Woodcock, who had an audience with the king, gave some outstanding examples in *South Sea Journey*, the book I carried with me, and some of the subsequent instances are even more memorable. For example, when the ticking began to grow loud on the countdown of Hong Kong's reversion to the People's Republic of China, the king instigated a policy of selling Tongan passports and nationality to panicky Hongkongese. There was no residency requirement, just cash. The scheme brought in considerable revenue, but ultimately backfired when friendly neighbouring countries such as Australia and New Zealand refused to recognize the new category of document. At one point, legitimate Tongan passports belonging to resident natives of Tonga were automatically viewed with extreme suspicion at airports round the world, just as happened with those of Nigeria when fraudulent and counterfeit Nigerian passports (a different matter entirely, of course) began triggering alarms at customs desks. While it lasted, however, the Tongan passport plan seemed like such a good idea that Kiribati, to the north, began a similar scheme. Tonga is fortunate to have been awarded the designation *.to* as its Internet domain. So now it is selling use of the suffix to foreign companies, such as an airline that has chosen "fly.to" and a maker of Italian foods that has selected "antipas.to." Such initiative prompted a resident of Pitcairn, a great-

great-great-grandson of the mutineer Fletcher Christian, to register *pn* as the island's Net domain, and then offer its use in e-mail addresses for a flat £100. One of the smallest players, Tuvalu, lying between Vanuatu and Kiribati, earned 10 per cent of its revenue in 1996 by selling its telephone country-code (688) to the operators of sex-lines in the U.S.

The Pacific island nations in such need of funds to support their rising populations realized their dilemma too late to become flags-of-convenience for the shipping industry; Panama and Liberia still dominate that market between them, and aren't bothered by the few crumbs of registration that fall to such places as the Isle of Man, the *Pride of Great Yarmouth*'s alma mater. South Pacific countries have, however, done a brisk business selling fishing licences to the fleets of the United States, Japan, Taiwan, and South Korea, though the profit is likely to be proscribed by the inevitable overfishing, a practice that already has ruined many sectors of the Atlantic fishery. This leaves money-laundering, though only the harshest critics of the region dare to utter the term in place of "offshore banking," the polite usage. Vanuatu is the longest established tax haven in the South Pacific, if not the most sophisticated. Port Vila has eighty private banks and a great many firms of lawyers, accountants, insurance agents, and the like, catering to the brass-plaque trade, so called because the brass nameplates on the door are often the foreign corporations' only physical asset in Vanuatu itself. The Cook Islands, Niue, Kiribati, Tuvalu, and Nauru are also in the same business. So in its way is Tonga. So is Western Samoa. The financial community in the last-named place has become more worldly than it was in 1990, when the government ordered new plastic

banknotes from the Reserve Bank of Australia, only to discover that the notes, designed to foil counterfeiters, did not
retain the ink used on the portrait of Malietoa Tanumafili II,
the head of state, whose likeness rubbed off in the hands of
alarmed Samoans.

Tonga isn't the only Pacific nation lying on or near the
International Date Line, which takes an unexpected east-
erly jog from the 180th degree of longitude. The northern
Fiji island of Taveuni sits astride the meridian and makes a
strong claim to being the spot where the sun will rise on the
first day of the new millennium. The Fiji National Millennium Commission is busy trying to milk the fact for all it
is worth. It finds itself, however, in competition with, for
example, the residents of Kiribati, who have renamed one
of their islands Millennium to enhance their assertion that
the first rays of January 1, 2000, will strike them – and the
thousands of well-heeled tourists expected to be on hand
to witness the event. Not taking any chances, Kiribati has
also leased land to the People's Republic of China, which
has built a large satellite tracking station. Its purpose is
primarily non-military, but western analysts feel that the
People's Liberation Army will use it as well. In that case,
China may have begun to bring its own style of military
build-up to the South Pacific, just as it has done to the
Indian Ocean.

I write these last few words on June 29, 1998, the day
when the death tally from piracy during the past twelve
months is released: the number is fifty-seven, a sharp
increase. This was also the day of the last tea auction in
London (the first took place in 1679). Before containeriza-
tion, tea from Asia was brought to London to be inspected

for water damage before coming under the auctioneer's gavel. Now there is no need for such on-site inspection. Accordingly, there is no need to buy and sell in person, gathered all together in one place, instead of on the Net. I make note of the date for a third reason as well. After six months back home, I have finally concluded that I need to take a further look at the changing South Pacific. God help me, I am looking for another ship.

❧

NOTE

The MV *Pride of Great Yarmouth* is a pastiche of more than one ship. Its officers, crew, and passengers, along with all other characters in my story, are composites. I have taken this traditional approach, following the recent footsteps of Christopher Buckley and so many others, in order to sharpen reality and spare people's feelings. Otherwise, as Mark Twain used to say, I have adhered to the perpendicular truth.

This book owes its existence to Neil Reynolds, the editor of the Ottawa *Citizen*. It is dedicated to the memory of Mark Seltzer (1957–98), a consummate traveller, who died tragically off Baffin Island.